interchange

FIFTH EDITION

1B

Student's Book

Jack C. Richards
with Jonathan Hull and Susan Proctor

WITH EBOOK

CAMBRIDGE
UNIVERSITY PRESS

CAMBRIDGE
UNIVERSITY PRESS

University Printing House, Cambridge CB2 8BS, United Kingdom

One Liberty Plaza, 20th Floor, New York, NY 10006, USA

477 Williamstown Road, Port Melbourne, VIC 3207, Australia

314–321, 3rd Floor, Plot 3, Splendor Forum, Jasola District Centre, New Delhi – 110025, India

103 Penang Road, #05-06/07, Visioncrest Commercial, Singapore 238467

Cambridge University Press is part of the University of Cambridge.

It furthers the University's mission by disseminating knowledge in the pursuit of education, learning and research at the highest international levels of excellence.

www.cambridge.org
Information on this title: www.cambridge.org/9781009040488

© Cambridge University Press 1991, 2017

First published 1991
Second edition 1997
Third edition 2005
Fourth edition 2013
Fifth edition 2017
Fifth edition update published 2022

20 19 18 17 16 15 14 13 12 11 10 9 8 7 6

Printed in Great Britain by CPI Group (UK) Ltd, Croydon CR0 4YY

A catalogue record for this publication is available from the British Library

ISBN 978-1-009-04044-0 Student's Book 1 with eBook
ISBN 978-1-009-04047-1 Student's Book 1A with eBook
ISBN 978-1-009-04048-8 Student's Book 1B with eBook
ISBN 978-1-009-04063-1 Student's Book 1 with Digital Pack
ISBN 978-1-009-04064-8 Student's Book 1A with Digital Pack
ISBN 978-1-009-04065-5 Student's Book 1B with Digital Pack
ISBN 978-1-316-62247-6 Workbook 1
ISBN 978-1-316-62254-4 Workbook 1A
ISBN 978-1-316-62266-7 Workbook 1B
ISBN 978-1-108-40606-2 Teacher's Edition 1
ISBN 978-1-316-62226-1 Class Audio 1
ISBN 978-1-009-04066-2 Full Contact 1 with Digital Pack
ISBN 978-1-009-04067-9 Full Contact 1A with Digital Pack
ISBN 978-1-009-04068-6 Full Contact 1B with Digital Pack
ISBN 978-1-108-40305-4 Presentation Plus Level 1

Additional resources for this publication at cambridgeone.org

Informed by teachers

Teachers from all over the world helped develop *Interchange Fifth Edition*. They looked at everything – from the color of the designs to the topics in the conversations – in order to make sure that this course will work in the classroom. We heard from 1,500 teachers in:

- Surveys
- Focus Groups
- In-Depth Reviews

We appreciate the help and input from everyone. In particular, we'd like to give the following people our special thanks:

Jader Franceschi, **Actúa Idiomas,** Bento Gonçalves, Rio Grande do Sul, Brazil

Juliana Dos Santos Voltan Costa, **Actus Idiomas,** São Paulo, Brazil

Ella Osorio, **Angelo State University,** San Angelo, TX, US

Mary Hunter, **Angelo State University,** San Angelo, TX, US

Mario César González, **Angloamericano de Monterrey, SC,** Monterrey, Mexico

Samantha Shipman, **Auburn High School,** Auburn, AL, US

Linda, **Bernick Language School,** Radford, VA, US

Dave Lowrance, **Bethesda University of California,** Yorba Linda, CA, US

Tajbakhsh Hosseini**, Bezmialem Vakif University,** Istanbul, Turkey

Dilek Gercek, **Bil English,** Izmir, Turkey

erkan kolat, **Biruni University, ELT,** Istanbul, Turkey

Nika Gutkowska, **Bluedata International,** New York, NY, US

Daniel Alcocer Gómez, **Cecati 92,** Guadalupe, Nuevo León, Mexico

Samantha Webb, **Central Middle School,** Milton-Freewater, OR, US

Verónica Salgado, **Centro Anglo Americano,** Cuernavaca, Mexico

Ana Rivadeneira Martínez and Georgia P. de Machuca, **Centro de Educación Continua – Universidad Politécnica del Ecuador,** Quito, Ecuador

Anderson Francisco Guimerães Maia, **Centro Cultural Brasil Estados Unidos,** Belém, Brazil

Rosana Mariano, **Centro Paula Souza,** São Paulo, Brazil

Carlos de la Paz Arroyo, Teresa Noemí Parra Alarcón, Gilberto

Bastida Gaytan, Manuel Esquivel Román, and Rosa Cepeda Tapia, **Centro Universitario Angloamericano,** Cuernavaca, Morelos, Mexico

Antonio Almeida, **CETEC,** Morelos, Mexico

Cinthia Ferreira, **Cinthia Ferreira Languages Services,** Toronto, ON, Canada

Phil Thomas and Sérgio Sanchez, **CLS Canadian Language School,** São Paulo, Brazil

Celia Concannon, **Cochise College,** Nogales, AZ, US

Maria do Carmo Rocha and CAOP English team, **Colégio Arquidiocesano Ouro Preto – Unidade Cônego Paulo Dilascio,** Ouro Preto, Brazil

Kim Rodriguez, **College of Charleston North,** Charleston, SC, US

Jesús Leza Alvarado, **Coparmex English Institute,** Monterrey, Mexico

John Partain, **Cortazar,** Guanajuato, Mexico

Alexander Palencia Navas, **Cursos de Lenguas, Universidad del Atlántico,** Barranquilla, Colombia

Kenneth Johan Gerardo Steenhuisen Cera, Melfi Osvaldo Guzman Triana, and Carlos Alberto Algarín Jiminez, **Cursos de Lenguas Extranjeras Universidad del Atlantico,** Barranquilla, Colombia

Jane P Kerford, **East Los Angeles College,** Pasadena, CA, US

Daniela, **East Village,** Campinas, São Paulo

Rosalva Camacho Orduño, **Easy English for Groups S.A. de C.V.,** Monterrey, Nuevo León, Mexico

Adonis Gimenez Fusetti, **Easy Way Idiomas,** Ibiúna, Brazil

Eileen Thompson, **Edison Community College,** Piqua, OH, US

Ahminne Handeri O.L Froede, **Englishouse escola de idiomas,** Teófilo Otoni, Brazil

Ana Luz Delgado-Izazola, **Escuela Nacional Preparatoria 5, UNAM,** Mexico City, Mexico

Nancy Alarcón Mendoza, **Facultad de Estudios Superiores Zaragoza, UNAM,** Mexico City, Mexico

Marcilio N. Barros, **Fast English USA,** Campinas, São Paulo, Brazil

Greta Douthat, **FCI Ashland,** Ashland, KY, US

Carlos Lizárraga González, **Grupo Educativo Anglo Americano, S.C.,** Mexico City, Mexico

Hugo Fernando Alcántar Valle, **Instituto Politécnico Nacional, Escuela Superior de Comercio y Administración-Unidad Santotomás, Celex Esca Santo Tomás,** Mexico City, Mexico

Sueli Nascimento, **Instituto Superior de Educação do Rio de Janeiro,** Rio de Janeiro, Brazil

Elsa F Monteverde, **International Academic Services,** Miami, FL, US

Laura Anand, **Irvine Adult School,** Irvine, CA, US

Prof. Marli T. Fernandes (principal) and Prof. Dr. Jefferson J. Fernandes (pedagogue), **Jefferson Idiomass,** São Paulo, Brazil

Herman Bartelen, **Kanda Gaigo Gakuin,** Tokyo, Japan

Cassia Silva, **Key Languages,** Key Biscayne, FL, US

Sister Mary Hope, **Kyoto Notre Dame Joshi Gakuin,** Kyoto, Japan

Nate Freedman, **LAL Language Centres,** Boston, MA, US

Richard Janzen, **Langley Secondary School,** Abbotsford, BC, Canada

Christina Abel Gabardo, **Language House,** Campo Largo, Brazil

Ivonne Castro, **Learn English International,** Cali, Colombia

Julio Cesar Maciel Rodrigues, **Liberty Centro de Línguas,** São Paulo, Brazil

Ann Gibson, **Maynard High School,** Maynard, MA, US

Martin Darling, **Meiji Gakuin Daigaku,** Tokyo, Japan

Dax Thomas, **Meiji Gakuin Daigaku,** Yokohama, Kanagawa, Japan

Derya Budak, **Mevlana University,** Konya, Turkey

B Sullivan, **Miami Valley Career Technical Center International Program,** Dayton, OH, US

Julio Velazquez, **Milo Language Center,** Weston, FL, US

Daiane Siqueira da Silva, Luiz Carlos Buontempo, Marlete Avelina de Oliveira Cunha, Marcos Paulo Segatti, Morgana Eveline de Oliveira, Nadia Lia Gino Alo, and Paul Hyde Budgen, **New Interchange-Escola de Idiomas,** São Paulo, Brazil

Patrícia França Furtado da Costa, Juiz de Fora, Brazil Patricia Servín

Chris Pollard, **North West Regional College SK,** North Battleford, SK, Canada

Olga Amy, **Notre Dame High School,** Red Deer, Canada

Amy Garrett, **Ouachita Baptist University,** Arkadelphia, AR, US

Mervin Curry, **Palm Beach State College,** Boca Raton, FL, US

Julie Barros, **Quality English Studio,** Guarulhos, São Paulo, Brazil

Teodoro González Saldaña and Jesús Monserrrta Mata Franco, **Race Idiomas,** Mexico City, Mexico

Autumn Westphal and Noga La`or, **Rennert International,** New York, NY, US

Antonio Gallo and Javy Palau, **Rigby Idiomas,** Monterrey, Mexico Tatiane Gabriela Sperb do Nascimento, **Right Way,** Igrejinha, Brazil

Mustafa Akgül, **Selahaddin Eyyubi Universitesi,** Diyarbakır, Turkey

James Drury M. Fonseca, **Senac Idiomas Fortaleza,** Fortaleza, Ceara, Brazil

Manoel Fialho S Neto, **Senac – PE,** Recife, Brazil

Jane Imber, **Small World,** Lawrence, KS, US

Tony Torres, **South Texas College,** McAllen, TX, US

Janet Rose, **Tennessee Foreign Language Institute,** College Grove, TN, US

Todd Enslen, **Tohoku University,** Sendai, Miyagi, Japan

Daniel Murray, **Torrance Adult School,** Torrance, CA, US

Juan Manuel Pulido Mendoza, **Universidad del Atlántico,** Barranquilla, Colombia

Juan Carlos Vargas Millán, **Universidad Libre Seccional Cali,** Cali (Valle del Cauca), Colombia

Carmen Cecilia Llanos Ospina, **Universidad Libre Seccional Cali,** Cali, Colombia

Jorge Noriega Zenteno, **Universidad Politécnica del Valle de México,** Estado de México, Mexico

Aimee Natasha Holguin S., **Universidad Politécnica del Valle de México UPVM,** Tultitlàn Estado de México, Mexico

Christian Selene Bernal Barraza, **UPVM Universidad Politécnica del Valle de México,** Ecatepec, Mexico

Lizeth Ramos Acosta, **Universidad Santiago de Cali,** Cali, Colombia

Silvana Dushku, **University of Illinois Champaign,** IL, US

Deirdre McMurtry, **University of Nebraska – Omaha,** Omaha, NE, US

Jason E Mower, **University of Utah,** Salt Lake City, UT, US

Paul Chugg, **Vanguard Taylor Language Institute,** Edmonton, Alberta, Canada

Henry Mulak, **Varsity Tutors,** Los Angeles, CA, US

Shirlei Strucker Calgaro and Hugo Guilherme Karrer, **VIP Centro de Idiomas,** Panambi, Rio Grande do Sul, Brazil

Eleanor Kelly, **Waseda Daigaku Extension Centre,** Tokyo, Japan

Sherry Ashworth, **Wichita State University,** Wichita, KS, US

Laine Bourdene, **William Carey University,** Hattiesburg, MS, US

Serap Aydın, Istanbul, Turkey

Liliana Covino, Guarulhos, Brazil

Yannuarys Jiménez, Barranquilla, Colombia

Juliana Morais Pazzini, Toronto, ON, Canada

Marlon Sanches, Montreal, Canada

Additional content contributed by Kenna Bourke, Inara Couto, Nic Harris, Greg Manin, Ashleigh Martinez, Laura McKenzie, Paul McIntyre, Clara Prado, Lynne Robertson, Mari Vargo, Theo Walker, and Maria Lucia Zaorob.

Plan of Book 1B

Pronunciation/Listening	Writing/Reading	Interchange Activity
Contrastive stress Listening to descriptions of people; identifying people	Writing an email describing a person "The Age of Selfies": Reading about the history of selfies	"Find the differences": Comparing two pictures of a party PAGES 123–124
Linked sounds Listening to descriptions of events	Writing an email to an old friend "Unique Experiences": Reading about four peoples' unusual experiences	"Fun survey": Finding out about a classmate's lifestyle PAGE 125
Can't and *shouldn't* Listening to descriptions of cities, towns, and countries	Writing about hometowns "A Big 'Hello!' From . . . ": Reading about interesting cities	"Welcome to our city!": Creating a guide to fun places in a city PAGE 126
Reduction of *to* Listening to health problems and advice	Writing a blog post "Toothache? Visit the Rain Forest!": Reading about a plant used as medicine	"What should I do?": Give suggestions for situations PAGE 127
Stress in responses Listening to restaurant orders	Writing a restaurant review "To Tip or Not to Tip?": Reading about tipping customs	"Planning a food festival": Creating a menu PAGE 128
Questions of choice Listening to a TV quiz show	Writing an article about a place "Earth's Cleanest Places": Reading about three very clean places	"How much do you know?": Taking a general knowledge quiz PAGE 129
Reduction of *could you* and *would you* Listening to telephone messages	Writing text message requests "Cell Phone Trouble!": Reading about cell phone problems	"Weekend plans": Finding out about classmates' weekend plans PAGE 130
Vowel sounds /oʊ/ and /ʌ/ Listening to descriptions of changes	Writing a plan for a class trip "A Goal Accomplished": Reading about a person's goals	"Our possible future": Planning a possible future PAGE 131

9 What does she look like?

▸ Describe people's physical appearance
▸ Identify people by describing how they look and what they're doing

1 WORD POWER Physical appearance

A Look at these expressions. What are three more words or expressions to describe people? Write them in the box below.

HAIR

| long brown hair | short blond hair | straight black hair | curly red hair | bald | a mustache and a beard |

AGE

| young | middle-aged | elderly |

LOOKS

| handsome | good-looking | pretty |

HEIGHT

| short | fairly short | medium height | pretty tall | very tall |

Other words or expressions
_____
_____
_____

B **PAIR WORK** Choose at least four expressions to describe yourself and your partner. Then compare. Do you agree?

A: You have long blond hair. You're pretty tall.
B: I don't think so. My hair isn't very long.

Me	My partner

2 CONVERSATION She's so pretty!

▶ **A** Listen and practice.

Lauren: I hear you have a new girlfriend, Justin.

Justin: Yes. Her name's Tiffany. She's really smart, and she's so pretty!

Lauren: Really? What does she look like?

Justin: Well, she's very tall.

Lauren: How tall?

Justin: About 5 foot 10, I suppose.

Lauren: Yeah, that *is* pretty tall. What color is her hair?

Justin: She has beautiful brown hair.

Lauren: And how old is she?

Justin: I don't know. I think it's a little rude to ask.

▶ **B** Listen to the rest of the conversation. What else do you learn about Tiffany?

3 GRAMMAR FOCUS

▶ **Describing people**

General appearance	Height	Hair	Age
What does she look like?	How tall is she?	How long is her hair?	How old is she?
She's tall, with brown hair.	She's 1 meter 78.	It's pretty short.	She's about 32.
She's pretty.	She's 5 foot 10.		She's in her thirties.
Does he wear glasses?	How tall is he?	What color is his hair?	How old is he?
No, he wears contacts.	He's medium height.	It's dark/light brown.	He's in his twenties.

Saying heights

	U.S.	Metric
	five (foot) ten.	one meter seventy-eight tall.
Tiffany is	five foot ten inches (tall).	1 meter 78.
	5'10".	178 cm.

GRAMMAR PLUS *see page 140*

A Write questions to match these statements. Then compare with a partner.

1. _____? My father is 52.
2. _____? I'm 167 cm (5 foot 6).
3. _____? My cousin has red hair.
4. _____? No, he wears contact lenses.
5. _____? He's tall and very good-looking.
6. _____? My sister's hair is medium length.
7. _____? I have dark brown eyes.

B PAIR WORK Choose a person in your class. Don't tell your partner who it is. Your partner will ask questions to guess the person's name.

A: Is it a man or a woman?   **A:** What color is his hair?

B: It's a man.   **B:** . . .

4 LISTENING Which one is Justin?

A Listen to descriptions of six people. Number them from 1 to 6.

B Listen again. How old is each person?

5 INTERCHANGE 9 Find the differences

Compare two pictures of a party. Student A go to Interchange 9A on page 123.
Student B go to Interchange 9B on page 124.

6 WRITING Describing physical appearance

A You are helping to organize a special event at your school with sports, arts,
and a surprise celebrity guest. Write an email to a friend inviting him or her
to the event, and describe the celebrity. Don't give the celebrity's name.

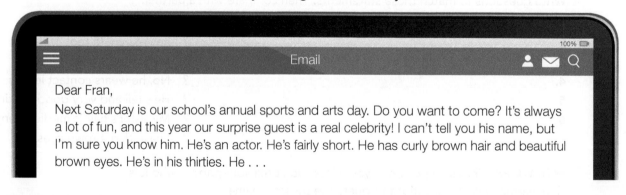

Dear Fran,
Next Saturday is our school's annual sports and arts day. Do you want to come? It's always a lot of fun, and this year our surprise guest is a real celebrity! I can't tell you his name, but I'm sure you know him. He's an actor. He's fairly short. He has curly brown hair and beautiful brown eyes. He's in his thirties. He . . .

B GROUP WORK Read your email to the group. Can they guess
the celebrity you are describing?

7 SNAPSHOT

New York *Street Fashion*

Boho (Bohemian)

The boho girl wears comfortable clothes – long skirts and flowy dresses in colorful floral prints.

Classic Prep

The preppy guy wears shirts and sweaters in pastel colors, khaki pants, and leather belts.

Hipster

The hipster wears hip hats, jewelry, and large glasses. Black is a popular color. The men often have unique hairstyles and long beards.

Streetwear

The streetwear fan wears casual and trendy clothes: jeans, basketball jerseys, baseball caps, T-shirts with logos, and cool sneakers.

Do you see your style(s)? Which one(s)?

Which style(s) do you like? Which do you dislike? Why?

Do you see any of these styles on the streets in your town or city? Which one(s)?

8 CONVERSATION Which one is she?

▶ **A** Listen and practice.

Brooke: Hi, Diego! Good to see you! Is Cora here, too?

Diego: Oh, she couldn't make it. She went to a concert with Alanna.

Brooke: Oh! Let's go talk to my friend Paula. She doesn't know anyone here.

Diego: Paula? Which one is she? Is she the woman wearing a long skirt over there?

Brooke: No, she's the tall one in jeans and a scarf. She's standing near the window.

Diego: OK. I'd like to meet her.

▶ **B** Listen to the rest of the conversation. Label Liam, Hina, Sierra, and Matt in the picture.

9 GRAMMAR FOCUS

> **Modifiers with present participles and prepositions**
>
> **Participles**
>
> | Who's Diego? | He's **the man** | **wearing** a blue shirt. |
> | Which one is Diego? | He's **the one** | **talking** to Brooke. |
>
> **Prepositions**
>
> | Who's Brooke? | She's **the woman** | **with** long black hair. |
> | Which one is Paula? | She's **the tall one** | **in** jeans. |
> | Who are the Harrisons? | They're **the people** | **next to** the window. |
> | Which ones are the Harrisons? | They're **the ones** | **on** the couch. |
>
> GRAMMAR PLUS see page 140

A Rewrite these statements using modifiers with participles or prepositions.

1. Kyle is the tall guy. He's wearing a yellow shirt and brown pants.
   <u>Kyle is the tall guy wearing a yellow shirt and brown pants.</u>

2. Mark and Eve are the middle-aged couple. They're talking to Michael.
   _____

3. Alexis is the young girl. She's in a white T-shirt and blue jeans.
   _____

4. Britney is the woman in the green dress. She's sitting to the left of Javier.
   _____

5. J.P. is the serious-looking boy. He's playing a video game.
   _____

B PAIR WORK Complete these questions using your classmates' names and information. Then take turns asking and answering the questions.

1. Who's the guy (man) sitting next to
   _____?

2. Who's the girl (woman) wearing
   _____?

3. Who is _____?
4. Which one is _____?
5. Who are the people _____?
6. Who are the ones _____?

10 PRONUNCIATION Contrastive stress in responses

A Listen and practice. Notice how the stress changes to emphasize a contrast.

A: Is Rob the one wearing the red shirt?

B: No, he's the one wearing the black shirt.

A: Is Rachel the woman on the couch?

B: No, Jen is the woman on the couch.

B Mark the stress changes in these conversations. Listen and check. Then practice the conversations.

A: Is Sophie the one sitting next to Judy?

B: No, she's the one standing next to Judy.

A: Is David the one on the couch?

B: No, he's the one behind the couch.

A Match the descriptions with the pictures. Write the letter.

This picture is out of this world! _____   An old idea meets the twenty-first century. _____

My life in fashion. _____   The real me or the "perfect" me? _____

THE AGE OF 🔄 SELFIES

THE BIRTH OF THE SELFIE

Most of us take selfies now and then. Presidents, rock stars, actors, and sports stars all take them. It's very easy to take selfies on a smartphone. But the selfie isn't really a new idea. Back in 1839, a man named Robert Cornelius took the very first selfie. Cornelius was a photographer from Philadelphia, in the U.S. He took the picture of himself by setting up his camera and then running to stand in front of it. On the back of the picture, Cornelius wrote: "The first light picture ever taken. 1839."

WORLD'S BEST SELFIE?

Astronaut Aki Hoshide is the third Japanese astronaut to walk in space. But that's not the only reason he's famous. Hoshide created an amazing image! The astronaut took this picture while he was at the International Space Station. The photo shows him, the sun, and deep space in the same shot. He named it "Orbiting Astronaut Self-Portrait."

THE PSYCHOLOGY OF SELFIES

Why do people want to take pictures of themselves? Psychologists say that it's a way of understanding who we are. It's also a way of controlling how other people see us. When we take selfies, we can choose the flattering ones – the ones that make us look really good – and share them with our friends on social media or over text. Some people take their selfies very seriously. There are even apps people can use to make their faces look "perfect."

THE DAILY SELFIE

Several years ago, Poppy Dinsey started a fashion blog. She had a simple but great idea. Every day for a year she posted a selfie of herself wearing a different outfit. So one day, she's wearing jeans. Another day, she's wearing skinny pants and a baggy sweater. The next day, she's wearing a hip dress. People loved Poppy's blog. Many people started their own fashion blogs because they liked her so much.

B Read the blog. Match each question with the correct answer.

1. What is Poppy Dinsey famous for? _____
2. Where did Aki Hoshide take a selfie? _____
3. Who says selfies are a way of understanding ourselves? _____
4. Who took the first selfie? _____
5. Where do many people post selfies? _____
6. What is Hoshide's job? _____

a. at the International Space Station
b. astronaut
c. on social media
d. psychologists
e. a fashion blog
f. a man from Philadelphia

C **PAIR WORK** What do you think of selfies? When and where do you take selfies? What's the main reason you take selfies?

What does she look like? 63

10 Have you ever been there?

▸ Describe recent activities
▸ Describe experiences from the recent and distant past

1 SNAPSHOT

Fun for everyone around Orlando!

☐ go to a theme park   ☐ go dancing   ☐ visit a space center   ☐ eat Cuban food   ☐ see an alligator

Which activities have you done?
Check (✓) the activities you would like to try.
Where can you do these or similar activities in your country?

2 CONVERSATION My feet are killing me!

▶ **A** Listen and practice.

Erin: It's great to see you again, Carlos! Have you been in Orlando long?

Carlos: You too, Erin! I've been here for about a week.

Erin: I can't wait to show you the city. Have you been to the theme parks yet?

Carlos: Yeah, I've already been to three. The lines were so long!

Erin: OK. Well, how about shopping? I know a great store. . .

Carlos: Well, I've already been to so many stores. I can't buy any more clothes.

Erin: I know what! I bet you haven't visited the Kennedy Space Center. It's an hour away.

Carlos: Actually, I've already been to the Space Center and met an astronaut!

Erin: Wow! You've done a lot! Well, is there anything you want to do?

Carlos: You know, I really just want to take it easy today. My feet are killing me!

▶ **B** Listen to the rest of the conversation. What do they plan to do tomorrow?

3 GRAMMAR FOCUS

▶ Present perfect; *already, yet*

The present perfect is formed with the verb *have* + the past participle.

Have you **been** to a jazz club?

Yes, I**'ve been** to several.   No, I **haven't been** to one.

Has Carlos **visited** the theme parks?

Yes, he**'s visited** three or four.   No, he **hasn't visited** any parks.

Have they **eaten** dinner yet?

Yes, they**'ve** already **eaten**.   No, they **haven't eaten** yet.

Contractions		
I**'ve**	=	I have
you**'ve**	=	you have
he**'s**	=	he has
she**'s**	=	she has
it**'s**	=	it has
we**'ve**	=	we have
they**'ve**	=	they have
has**n't**	=	has not
have**n't**	=	have not

GRAMMAR PLUS *see page 141*

A How many times have you done these things in the past week? Write your answers. Then compare with a partner.

1. cook dinner
2. wash the dishes
3. listen to music
4. do the laundry
5. go to a restaurant
6. clean the house

> I've cooked dinner twice this week.
>
> OR
>
> I haven't cooked dinner this week.

regular past participles		
visit	→	visited
like	→	liked
stop	→	stopped
try	→	tried

irregular past participles		
be	→	been
do	→	done
eat	→	eaten
go	→	gone
have	→	had
hear	→	heard
make	→	made
ride	→	ridden
see	→	seen

B Complete these conversations using the present perfect. Then practice with a partner.

1. **A:** _____Have_____ you _____done_____ much exercise this week? (do)

   B: Yes, I _____ already _____ to Pilates class four times. (be)

2. **A:** _____ you _____ any sports this month? (play)

   B: No, I _____ the time. (not have)

3. **A:** How many movies _____ you _____ to this month? (be)

   B: Actually, I _____ any yet. (not see)

4. **A:** _____ you _____ to any interesting parties recently? (be)

   B: No, I _____ to any parties for quite a while. (not go)

5. **A:** _____ you _____ any food this week? (cook)

   B: Yes, I _____ already _____ dinner twice. (make)

6. **A:** How many times _____ you _____ out to eat this week? (go)

   B: I _____ at fast-food restaurants a couple of times. (eat)

C PAIR WORK Take turns asking the questions in part B. Give your own information when answering.

4 CONVERSATION Have you ever had a Cuban sandwich?

▶ **A** Listen and practice.

Erin: I'm sorry I'm late. Have you been here long?

Carlos: No, only for a few minutes. So, have you chosen a restaurant yet?

Erin: I can't decide. We can go to a big restaurant or a have a sandwich at a café. Have you ever had a Cuban sandwich?

Carlos: No, I haven't. Are they good?

Erin: They're delicious. I've had them many times.

Carlos: You really like Cuban food! Have you ever been to Cuba?

Erin: No, but I went to college in Miami. I ate empanadas and rice and beans all the time!

▶ **B** Listen to the rest of the conversation. Where do they decide to go after lunch?

5 GRAMMAR FOCUS

▶
Present perfect vs. simple past		
	Use the present perfect for an indefinite time in the past.	**Use the simple past for a specific event in the past.**
Have you ever **eaten** Cuban food?	Yes, I **have**. I**'ve had** it many times. No, I **haven't**. I **haven't tried** it yet.	I **ate** a lot of Cuban food when I **lived** in Miami. No, I never **tried** it when I **lived** in Miami.
Have you ever **seen** an alligator?	Yes, I **have**. I**'ve seen** a few alligators in my life. No, I **haven't**. I**'ve** never **seen** one.	I **saw** a big alligator at the new park last week. I **didn't go** to the alligator park last week, so I **didn't see** any.

GRAMMAR PLUS *see page 141*

A Complete these conversations. Use the present perfect and simple past of the verbs given and short answers.

1. A: _____ you ever _____ in public? (sing)

　　B: Yes, I _____ . I _____ at a friend's birthday party.

2. A: _____ you ever _____ something valuable? (lose)

　　B: No, I _____ . But my brother _____ his cell phone on a trip once.

3. A: _____ you ever _____ a traffic ticket? (get)

　　B: Yes, I _____ . Once I _____ a ticket and had to pay $50.

4. A: _____ you ever _____ a live concert? (see)

　　B: Yes, I _____ . I _____ Adele at the stadium last year.

5. A: _____ you ever _____ late for an important event? (be)

　　B: No, I _____ . But my sister _____ two hours late for her wedding!

B **PAIR WORK** Take turns asking the questions in part A. Give your own information when answering.

For and since

How long **did** you **live** in Miami?	I **lived** there **for** four years. It was a great experience.
How long **have** you **lived** in Orlando?	I**'ve lived** here **for** three years. I'm very happy here.
	I**'ve worked** at the hotel **since** last year. I love it there.

GRAMMAR PLUS *see page 141*

C Complete these sentences with *for* or *since*. Then compare with a partner.

1. Maura was in Central America _____ a month last year.
2. I've been a college student _____ almost four years.
3. Hiroshi has been at work _____ 6:00 A.M.
4. I haven't gone to a party _____ a long time.
5. Sean lived in Bolivia _____ two years as a kid.
6. My parents have been on vacation _____ Monday.
7. Jennifer was engaged to Theo _____ six months.
8. Alex and Brianna have been best friends _____ high school.

expressions with *for*

two weeks
a few months
several years
a long time

expressions with *since*

6:45
last weekend
2009
elementary school

D **PAIR WORK** Ask and answer these questions.

How long have you had your current hairstyle?
How long have you studied at this school?
How long have you known your best friend?
How long have you been awake today?

6 PRONUNCIATION Linked sounds

A Listen and practice. Notice how final /t/ and /d/ sounds in verbs are linked to the vowels that follow them.

A: Have you cooked lunch yet?
/t/
B: Yes, I've already cooked it.

A: Have you ever tried Key Lime Pie?
/d/
B: Yes, I tried it once in Miami.

B **PAIR WORK** Ask and answer these questions. Use *it* in your responses. Pay attention to the linked sounds.

Have you ever cut your own hair?
Have you ever tasted blue cheese?
Have you ever tried Vietnamese food?
Have you ever lost your ID?
Have you looked at Unit 11 yet?

7 LISTENING Great to see you!

Listen to Nicole tell Tyler about some interesting things she's done recently. Complete the chart.

Places Nicole went	What she did there	Has Tyler been there before?	
1.		☐ Yes	☐ No
2.		☐ Yes	☐ No

8 WORD POWER Life experiences

A Find two phrases to go with each verb. Write them in the chart.

| a bike | your English books | a costume | a truck | your phone | a motorcycle |
| sushi | chocolate soda | iced coffee | octopus | a sports car | a uniform |

eat	_____	_____	_____
drink	_____	_____	_____
drive	_____	_____	_____
lose	_____	_____	_____
ride	_____	_____	_____
wear	_____	_____	_____

B Add another phrase for each verb in part A.

9 SPEAKING Have you ever . . . ?

A **GROUP WORK** Ask your classmates questions about the activities in Exercise 8 or your own ideas.

A: Have you ever worn a costume?
B: Yes, I have.
C: Really? Where were you?

B **CLASS ACTIVITY** Tell the class one interesting thing you learned about a classmate.

10 WRITING An email to an old friend

A Write an email to someone you haven't seen for a long time. Include three things you've done since you last saw that person.

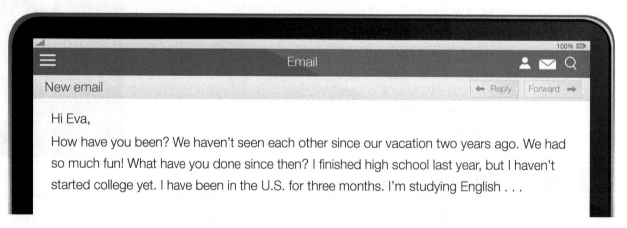

Hi Eva,

How have you been? We haven't seen each other since our vacation two years ago. We had so much fun! What have you done since then? I finished high school last year, but I haven't started college yet. I have been in the U.S. for three months. I'm studying English . . .

B **PAIR WORK** Exchange emails with a partner. Write a response about the three things your partner has done.

11 INTERCHANGE 10 Fun survey

How much fun do you have? Go to Interchange 10 on page 125.

A Look at the photos. Skim the blog posts. What did Jennifer Aniston do in her sleep? How did Mervyn Kincaid cross the Irish Sea?

UNIQUE EXPERIENCES

How much is that pizza?!

Do you like pizza? Do you *really* like pizza? Do you like pizza enough to spend over $100 on one? Some people do! And here's the reason why. Truffles are similar to mushrooms, but they grow underground. They're extremely expensive. They can cost hundreds of dollars each. Pizza usually only costs a few dollars, but some people have paid as much as $178 to eat pizza with fresh white truffles on it. Celebrity TV chef Gordon Ramsay has won a place in the Guinness Book of Records for inventing this expensive dish.

Do you sleepwalk?

Did you know that some people walk in their sleep? Well, you probably do because it's a surprisingly common problem. In fact, almost a third of the U.S. population has sleepwalked at some point in their lives. The actress Jennifer Aniston is one of them. Jennifer has set off the burglar alarm in her own house by walking around while she was asleep.

Set sail in a bathtub!

Have you ever dreamed of going on a really big adventure? One man has crossed the Irish Sea . . . in a bathtub! Yes, you heard that right. Mervyn Kincaid has sailed from Ireland to Scotland in a bathtub with a small engine attached. Even better, Mervyn has raised a lot of money for charity. His friends and family have all made donations.

Oh no! I hit "send"!

Have you ever pushed "send" on a text message and then realized you've just sent a text to the wrong person? Hopefully not! But Burt Brown has. This 30-year-old software engineer has just sent 30 cute pictures of his baby to his boss instead of his mom! Luckily, his boss is a good guy and understood the mistake.

B Read the blog posts. Check (✓) True or False.

	True	False
1. Pizza is very expensive in the U.S.	☐	☐
2. Truffles grow underground.	☐	☐
3. Mervyn Kincaid didn't use a boat for his journey.	☐	☐
4. Mervyn Kincaid crossed the Irish Sea to pay for his bathtub.	☐	☐
5. Sleepwalking is extremely rare.	☐	☐
6. There was a lot of noise when Jennifer Aniston walked in her sleep.	☐	☐
7. Burt Brown sent photos to his boss.	☐	☐
8. Burt's boss was very angry about the baby pictures.	☐	☐

C **GROUP WORK** What unique experiences have you had in your life? Were they fun? Were they embarrassing? Tell your classmates.

Units 9–10 Progress check

SELF-ASSESSMENT

How well can you do these things? Check (✓) the boxes.

I can . . .	Very well	OK	A little
Ask about and describe people's appearance (Ex. 1)	☐	☐	☐
Identify people by describing what they're doing, what they're wearing, and where they are (Ex. 2)	☐	☐	☐
Find out whether or not things have been done (Ex. 3)	☐	☐	☐
Understand descriptions of experiences (Ex. 4)	☐	☐	☐
Ask and answer questions about experiences (Ex. 4)	☐	☐	☐
Find out how long people have done things (Ex. 5)	☐	☐	☐

1 ROLE PLAY Missing person

Student A: One of your classmates is lost. You are talking to a police officer. Answer the officer's questions and describe your classmate.

Student B: You are a police officer. Someone is describing a lost classmate. Ask questions to complete the form. Can you identify the classmate?

Change roles and try the role play again.

> MISSING PERSON REPORT
> NAME _____
> HEIGHT: _____ WEIGHT: _____ AGE: _____
>
> EYE COLOR:
> ☐ BLUE ☐ BROWN
> ☐ GREEN ☐ HAZEL
>
> HAIR COLOR:
> ☐ BLOND ☐ BROWN
> ☐ RED ☐ BLACK
> ☐ GRAY ☐ BALD
>
> CLOTHING: _____
> _____
>
> GLASSES, ETC: _____

2 SPEAKING Which one is . . . ?

A Look at this picture. How many sentences can you write to identify the people?

> Mia and Derek are the people
> in sunglasses.
> They're the ones looking at the tablet.

B PAIR WORK Try to memorize the people in the picture. Then close your books. Take turns asking about the people.

A: Which one is Allen?
B: I think Allen is the guy eating . . .

3 SPEAKING "To do" lists

A Imagine you are preparing for these situations. Make a list of four things you need to do for each situation.

You are going to go to the beach this weekend.
Your first day of school is in a week.
You are going to move to a new apartment.

"To do" list: trip to the beach

1. buy a swimsuit

B **PAIR WORK** Exchange lists. Take turns asking about what has been done. When answering, decide what you have or haven't done.

A: Have you bought a swimsuit yet?
B: Yes, I've already gotten one.

4 LISTENING I won a contest!

A Alyssa has just met a friend in San Diego. Listen to her talk about things she has done. Check (✓) the correct things.

Alyssa has . . .

☐ won a contest.	☐ gone windsurfing.
☐ flown in a plane.	☐ lost her wallet.
☐ stayed in an expensive hotel.	☐ gotten sunburned.
☐ met a famous person.	☐ posted on a blog.

B **GROUP WORK** Have you ever done the things in part A? Take turns asking about each thing.

5 SURVEY How long have you . . .?

A Add one more question to the chart. Write answers to these questions using *for* and *since*.

How long have you . . . ?	My answers	Classmate's name
owned this book		
studied English		
known your teacher		
lived in this town or city		
been a student		
_____		

B **CLASS ACTIVITY** Go around the class. Find someone who has the same answers. Write a classmate's name only once.

WHAT'S NEXT?

Look at your Self-assessment again. Do you need to review anything?

It's a really nice city.

- ▸ Describe hometowns, cities, and countries
- ▸ Make recommendations about places to visit

1 WORD POWER Adjectives to describe places

A PAIR WORK Match each word in column A with its opposite in column B. Then add two more pairs of adjectives to the list.

A	B
1. beautiful	**a.** boring
2. cheap	**b.** crowded
3. clean	**c.** dangerous
4. interesting	**d.** expensive
5. quiet	**e.** noisy
6. relaxing	**f.** polluted
7. safe	**g.** stressful
8. spacious	**h.** ugly
9. _____	**i.** _____
10. _____	**j.** _____

beautiful

B PAIR WORK Choose two places you know. Describe them to your partner using the words in part A.

ugly

2 CONVERSATION It looks so relaxing.

▶ **A** Listen and practice.

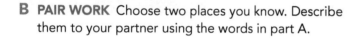

Ron That photo is really cool! Where is that?

Camila That's a beach near my house in Punta Cana, in the Dominican Republic.

Ron It looks so relaxing. I've heard the area is really beautiful.

Camila Yeah, it is. The weather is great, and there are some fantastic beaches. The water is really clear, too.

Ron Is it expensive there?

Camila Well, it's not cheap. But prices for tourists can be pretty reasonable.

Ron Hmm . . . and how far is it from Santo Domingo?

Camila It's not *too* far from the capital. About 200 kilometers . . . a little over 120 miles.

Ron It sounds very interesting. I should plan a trip there sometime.

▶ **B** Listen to the rest of the conversation. What does Camila say about entertainment in Punta Cana?

Punta Cana, Dominican Republic

3 GRAMMAR FOCUS

▶ **Adverbs before adjectives**

		adverbs
Punta Cana is **really** nice.	It's a **really** nice place.	too
It's **fairly** expensive.	It's a **fairly** expensive destination.	extremely
It's not **very** big.	It's not a **very** big city.	very/really
New York is **too** noisy, and it's **too** crowded for me.		pretty
	GRAMMAR PLUS *see page 142*	fairly/somewhat

A Match the questions with the answers. Then practice the conversations with a partner.

1. What's Seoul like? Is it an interesting place? _____
2. Do you like your hometown? Why or why not? _____
3. What's Sydney like? I've never been there. _____
4. Have you ever been to São Paulo? _____
5. What's the weather like in Chicago? _____

a. Oh, really? It's beautiful and very clean. It has a great harbor and beautiful beaches.
b. Yes, I have. It's an extremely large and crowded place, but I love it. It has excellent restaurants.
c. It's really nice in the summer, but it's too cold for me in the winter.
d. Not really. It's too small, and it's really boring. That's why I moved away.
e. Yes. It has amazing shopping, and the people are pretty friendly.

▶ **Conjunctions**

Los Angeles is a big city, **and** the weather is nice.	It's a big city. It's not too big, **though**.
Boston is a big city, **but** it's not too big.	It's a big city. It's not too big, **however**.
	GRAMMAR PLUS *see page 142*

B Choose the correct conjunctions and rewrite the sentences.

1. Kyoto is very nice. Everyone is extremely friendly. (and / but)

   _____

2. The streets are crowded during the day. They're very quiet at night. (and / though)

   _____

3. The weather is nice. Summers get pretty hot. (and / however)

   _____

4. You can rent a bicycle. It's expensive. (and / but)

   _____

5. It's an amazing city. I love to go there. (and / however)

   _____

C GROUP WORK Describe three cities or towns in your country. State two positive features and one negative feature for each.

A: Singapore is very exciting and there are a lot of things to do, but it's too expensive.

B: The weather in Bogotá is . . .

Kyoto, Japan

It's a really nice city. **73**

4 LISTENING Describing hometowns

▶ **A** Listen to Abby and Christopher talk about their hometowns.
What do they say about them? Choose the correct words.

Abby's hometown	Christopher's hometown
a fairly / not very large town	a really / fairly stressful place
somewhat / extremely beautiful	pretty / too crowded
pretty / very cheap	not very / extremely clean
_____ quiet	_____ expensive

▶ **B** Listen again. Write another adverb you hear them use to describe their hometowns.

5 WRITING A great place to live

A Write about interesting places for tourists to visit in your hometown.

> Otavalo is a very interesting town in Ecuador. It's to the north of Quito.
> It has a fantastic market, and a lot of tourists go there to buy handmade
> art and crafts. The scenery around Otavalo is very pretty and . . .

B **PAIR WORK** Exchange papers and read each other's articles.
What did you learn about your partner's hometown?

6 SNAPSHOT

SIX WORLD-FAMOUS LANDMARKS

1 The Grand Canyon Arizona, U.S. ☐

2 The Louvre Paris, France ☐

3 The pyramids Giza, Egypt ☐

4 The Colosseum Rome, Italy ☐

5 Sugarloaf Mountain Rio de Janeiro, Brazil ☐

6 Taj Mahal Agra, India ☐

Which places would you like to visit? Why?
Put the places you would like to visit in order from most interesting (1) to least interesting (6).
Which interesting places around your country or the world have you already visited?
What three other places around the world would you like to visit? Why?

7 CONVERSATION What should I do there?

▶ **A** Listen and practice.

JASON Can you tell me a little about Mexico City?

CLAUDIA Sure. What would you like to know?

JASON Well, I'm going to be there for a few days next month. What should I do there?

CLAUDIA Oh! You should definitely visit the National Museum of Anthropology. It's amazing.

JASON OK. It's on my list now! Anything else?

CLAUDIA You shouldn't miss the Diego Rivera murals. They're incredible. Oh, and you can walk around the historic center.

JASON That sounds perfect. And what about the food? What should I eat?

CLAUDIA You can't miss the street food. The tacos, barbecue, fruit . . . it's all delicious.

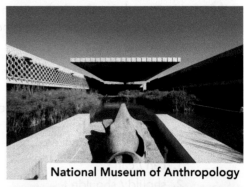
National Museum of Anthropology

Diego Rivera murals

▶ **B** Listen to the rest of the conversation. Where is Jason from? What should you do there?

8 GRAMMAR FOCUS

▶ **Modal verbs *can* and *should***

What **can** I do in Mexico City?	What **should** I see there?
You **can** walk around the historic center.	You **should** visit the National Museum of Anthropology.
You **can't** miss the street food.	You **shouldn't** miss the Diego Rivera murals.

GRAMMAR PLUS *see page 142*

A Complete these conversations using *can, can't, should,* or *shouldn't*. Then practice with a partner.

1. A: I _____ decide where to go on my vacation.
   B: You _____ go to Morocco. It's my favorite place to visit.

2. A: I'm planning to go to Puerto Rico next year. When do you think I _____ go?
   B: You _____ go anytime. The weather is nice almost all year.

3. A: _____ I rent a car when I arrive in New York? What do you recommend?
   B: No, you _____ definitely use the subway. It's fast and not too expensive.

4. A: Where _____ I get some nice jewelry in Istanbul?
   B: You _____ miss the Grand Bazaar. It's the best place for bargains.

5. A: What _____ I see from the Eiffel Tower?
   B: You _____ see all of Paris, but in bad weather, you _____ see anything.

B Write answers to these questions about your country. Then compare with a partner.

What time of year should you go there?   What can you do for free?
What are three things you can do there?   What shouldn't a visitor miss?

9 PRONUNCIATION *Can't and shouldn't*

▷ **A** Listen and practice these statements. Notice how the *t* in **can't** and **shouldn't** is not strongly pronounced.

You can get a taxi easily.
You can't get a taxi easily.
You should visit in the summer.
You shouldn't visit in the summer.

Las Vegas, United States

▷ **B** Listen to four sentences. Choose the modal verb you hear.

1. can / can't
2. should / shouldn't
3. can / can't
4. should / shouldn't

10 LISTENING Where should you go?

▷ **A** Listen to speakers talk about three countries. Complete the chart.

Country	Largest city	What visitors should see or do
1. Japan		
2.		
3.		

▷ **B** Listen again. What else do the speakers say about the countries?

11 SPEAKING What can visitors do there?

GROUP WORK Has anyone visited an interesting place in your country or in another country? Find out more about it. Start like this and ask questions like the ones below.

A: I visited Jeju Island once.
B: Really? What's the best time of year to visit?
A: Springtime is very nice. I went in May.
C: What's the weather like then?

What's the best time of year to visit?
What's the weather like then?
What should tourists see and do there?
What special foods can you eat?
What's the shopping like?
What things should people buy?
What else can visitors do there?

Jeju Island, South Korea

12 INTERCHANGE 11 Welcome to our city!

Make a guide to fun places in your city. Go to Interchange 11 on page 126.

A Skim the emails. What city is famous for small plates of food? Where is a good place to ride your bike at night?

A big "Hello!" from . . .

New mail ✉ Barcelona, Spain ← Reply | Forward → | ✕

Barcelona is simply awesome! The city is famous for the architect Antoni Gaudí. I've seen a different Gaudí building every day. Gaudí designed some amazing places like the church *La Sagrada Familia*. Workers started building the church in 1882, but it isn't finished yet. Some people say it might be finished by 2030. I've also visited *Las Ramblas*, a street with great cafés. I've eaten delicious tapas every day. A *tapa* is a small plate of food. My friends and I usually order several tapas and share them. The weather is great! I think I came here at just the right time of the year.

Kathy

New mail ✉ Cartagena, Colombia ← Reply | Forward → | ✕

I've discovered that Cartagena has two different personalities. One is a lively city with fancy restaurants and crowded old plazas. And the other is a quiet and relaxing place with sandy beaches. If you come here, you should stay in the historic district – a walled area with great shopping, nightclubs, and restaurants. It has some wonderful old Spanish buildings. Last night I learned some salsa steps at an old dance club. Today, I went on a canoe tour of *La Ciénaga* mangrove forest.

Mike

New mail ✉ Bangkok, Thailand ← Reply | Forward → | ✕

Bangkok is the most exciting place I've ever visited. There's something for everyone. You can surf or swim with sharks. Or why not try out some extreme cycling at Peppermint Bike Park? The park has two great bike paths. You can ride your bike there until 10:00 at night. I ate the most delicious food in Bangkok, including the famous pad thai – a spicy noodle dish. At night, there are clubs, restaurants, cafés, and movie theaters to visit. It's impossible to be bored. I love it!

Jasmin

B Read the emails. Check (✓) the cities where you can do these things. Then complete the chart with examples from the emails.

Activity	Barcelona	Cartagena	Bangkok	Examples
1. swim with sharks	☐	☐	☐	
2. see a famous church	☐	☐	☐	
3. eat spicy food	☐	☐	☐	
4. go dancing	☐	☐	☐	
5. take a boat tour	☐	☐	☐	
6. eat small plates of local food	☐	☐	☐	

C **PAIR WORK** Which city is the most interesting to you? Why? Which other city or cities in the world would you like to visit? Why?

12 It's important to get rest.

▸ State health problems and give advice
▸ Ask for advice and give suggestions about health products

1 SNAPSHOT

Common Health Problems

☐ a headache   ☐ a cough   ☐ a cold   ☐ the flu

☐ a stomachache   ☐ a backache   ☐ sore muscles   ☐ insomnia

How many times have you been sick in the past year?
Check (✓) the health problems you have had recently.
What do you do for the health problems you checked?

2 CONVERSATION It really works!

▶ **A** Listen and practice.

Mila: Are you all right, Keith?
Keith: Not really. I don't feel so well. I have a terrible cold.
Mila: Oh, that's too bad. You shouldn't be at the gym, then.
Keith: Yeah, I know. But I need to run for an hour every day.
Mila: Not today, Keith! It's really important to get some rest.
Keith: Yeah, you're right. I should be in bed.
Mila: Well, yeah! And have you taken anything for your cold?
Keith: No, I haven't. What should I take?
Mila: Well, you know, pain medicine, lots of water. Sometimes it's helpful to drink garlic tea. Just chop up some garlic and boil it for a few minutes, then add lemon and honey. Try it! It really works!
Keith: Yuck! That sounds awful!

▶ **B** Listen to advice from Keith's next-door neighbors. What do they suggest?

3 GRAMMAR FOCUS

▶ **Adjective + infinitive; noun + infinitive**

What should you do for a cold?	It's **important**	**to get** some rest.
	It's sometimes **helpful**	**to drink** garlic tea.
	It's **a good idea**	**to take** some vitamin C.

GRAMMAR PLUS *see page 143*

A Look at these health problems. Choose several pieces of good advice for each problem.

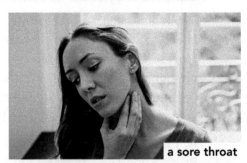
a sore throat

Problems
1. a backache _____
2. a bad headache _____
3. a burn _____
4. a cough _____
5. a fever _____
6. the flu _____
7. a sore throat _____
8. a toothache _____

Advice
a. drink lots of liquids
b. get some medicine
c. go to bed and rest
d. put it under cold water
e. put a heating pad on it
f. put some cream on it
g. see a dentist
h. see a doctor
i. take some pain medicine
j. take some vitamin C

a fever

B GROUP WORK Talk about the problems in part A and give advice. What other advice do you have?

A: What should you do for a backache?
B: It's a good idea to put a heating pad on it.
C: It's also important to see a doctor and . . .

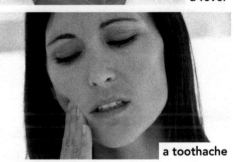
a toothache

C Write advice for these problems. (You will use this advice in Exercise 4.)

| an earache | a cold | a sunburn | sore muscles |

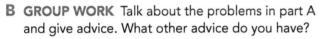

For an earache, it's a good idea to . . .

a burn

4 PRONUNCIATION Reduction of *to*

▶ **A** Listen and practice. In conversation, **to** is often reduced to /tə/.

A: What should you do for a toothache?
B: It's sometimes helpful **to** take some pain medicine. And it's important **to** see a dentist.

B PAIR WORK Look back at Exercise 3, part C. Ask for and give advice about each health problem. Pay attention to the pronunciation of **to**.

5 INTERCHANGE 12 What should I do?

Play a board game. Go to Interchange 12 on page 127.

6 DISCUSSION Good advice

A GROUP WORK Imagine these situations are true for you.
Get three suggestions for each one from your partners.

I sometimes feel really stressed.
I need to study, but I can't concentrate.
I feel sick before every exam.
I forget about half the new words I learn.
I get nervous when I speak English to foreigners.
I get really hungry before I go to bed.

A: I sometimes feel really stressed. What should I do?
B: It's a good idea to take a hot bath.
C: It's sometimes helpful to go for a walk.

B CLASS ACTIVITY Have any of the above situations
happened to you recently? Share what you did with
the class.

7 WORD POWER Containers

A Use the words in the list to complete these expressions.
Then compare with a partner. Sometimes more
than one answer is correct.

bag	jar
bottle	pack
box	stick
can	tube

1. a _____ of pain medicine
2. a _____ of bandages
3. a _____ of cough drops
4. a _____ of deodorant
5. a _____ of face cream
6. a _____ of shaving cream
7. a _____ of tissues
8. a _____ of toothpaste

B PAIR WORK What is one more thing you can
buy in each of the containers above?

"You can buy a bag of breath mints."

C PAIR WORK What are the five most useful
items in your medicine cabinet?

8 CONVERSATION Can you suggest anything?

▶ **A** Listen and practice.

Pharmacist: Hi. May I help you?

Mr. Peters: Yes, please. Could I have something for a backache? My muscles are really sore.

Pharmacist: Well, it's a good idea to use a heating pad. And why don't you try this cream? It works really well.

Mr. Peters: OK, I'll take one tube. Also, my wife has a bad cough. Can you suggest anything?

Pharmacist: She should try these cough drops.

Mr. Peters: Thanks! May I have a large bag? And what do you suggest for insomnia?

Pharmacist: Well, you could get a box of chamomile tea. Is it for you?

Mr. Peters: Yes, I can't sleep.

Pharmacist: A sore back and your wife's bad cough? I think I know why you can't sleep!

▶ **B** Listen to the pharmacist talk to the next customer. What does the customer want?

9 GRAMMAR FOCUS

▶ **Modal verbs *can*, *could*, and *may* for requests; suggestions**

Can/May I help you?	What do you suggest/have for a backache?
Can I have a bag of cough drops?	You could try this new cream.
Could I have something for a cough?	You should get a heating pad.
May I have a bottle of pain medicine?	Why don't you try these pills?

GRAMMAR PLUS *see page 143*

Choose the correct words. Then compare and practice with a partner.

1. **A: Can / Could** I help you?
   B: What do you **suggest / try** for dry skin?
   A: Why don't you **suggest / try** this lotion? It's excellent.
   B: OK. I'll take it.

2. **A: May / Do** I have something for itchy eyes?
   B: Sure. You **could / may** try a bottle of eyedrops.

3. **A:** Could I **suggest / have** a box of bandages, please?
   B: Here you are.
   A: And what do you **suggest / try** for insomnia?
   B: You **should / may** try this herbal tea. It's very relaxing.
   A: OK. Thanks.

10 LISTENING What's wrong?

▶ Listen to four people talking about problems and giving advice. Write the problem and the advice.

	Problem	Advice
1. John		
2. Ashley		
3. Brandon		
4. Rachel		

11 ROLE PLAY Can I help you?

Student A: You are a customer in a drugstore. You need:

something for a backache
something for dry skin
something for the flu
something for low energy
something for sore feet
something for an upset stomach

Ask for some suggestions.

Student B: You are a pharmacist in a drugstore.
A customer needs some things.
Make some suggestions.

Change roles and try the role play again.

12 WRITING Reacting to a blog post

A Read this health and fitness blog post on how to avoid stress.

Home	About	Healthy living	🔍

Suggestions for a Relaxing Life
Tuesday, March 29   healthyandhappy

Can we avoid stress in our lives? What should we do to have a relaxing life?
Everyone wants the answers to these questions. Well, we have a few suggestions:

* We should not work long hours or work on our days off.
* We should try to exercise three or four times a week.
* It's a good idea to buy only the things we really need.
* It's really important to have fun. Fun is the perfect remedy for stress!

B Now imagine you have your own blog. Write a post with your ideas on how to reduce stress and have a relaxing life. Think of an interesting name for your blog.

C GROUP WORK Exchange blog posts. Read your partners' blogs and write a suggestion at the bottom of each post. Then share the most interesting blog and suggestions with the class.

A Skim the article. Then check the best description of the article.

☐ The article gives the author's opinion about the subject.
☐ The article gives information and facts.
☐ The article tells a story about a scientist.

Toothache?
Visit the rain forest!

acmella oleracea

A Nobody likes having a toothache, and not many people enjoy visiting the dentist's office. Exciting new research suggests that there is a different way to treat a toothache – one that doesn't need an appointment with a dentist.

B Scientists say that a very rare red and yellow plant from the Amazon rain forest could stop a toothache. It's more powerful than taking pain medicine, and it's more effective than most treatments you get in the dentist's chair. The plant, named *acmella oleracea,* has been used as a remedy for toothaches by the Keshwa Lamas, a Peruvian community, for many years.

C Dr. Françoise Barbira Freedman is an anthropologist – a scientist who studies humans. She learned about the plant 30 years ago on a trip to Peru. One day, she got a terrible toothache. The people in the village where she was living gave her the remedy and her pain disappeared.

D Now this amazing plant has been made into a gel. Many tests show that it really helps with the pain of toothaches and even helps babies who are getting their first teeth. To thank the Keshwa Lamas for this remedy, there is a plan to give some of the money from the gel back to the community. So it's good news for everyone.

B Read the article. Then answer these questions. Write the letter of the paragraph where you find the answers.

1. _____ When did Dr. Freedman learn about the plant?
2. _____ What has the plant been made into?
3. _____ What is the plant's scientific name?
4. _____ Who gave Dr. Freedman the remedy?
5. _____ What will be given back to the Keshwa Lamas?
6. _____ Where can you find the plant?

C GROUP WORK What are some other reasons why rain forests are important?

Units 11–12 Progress check

SELF-ASSESSMENT

How well can you do these things? Check (✓) the boxes.

I can . . .	Very well	OK	A little
Understand descriptions of towns and cities (Ex. 1)	☐	☐	☐
Get useful information about towns and cities (Ex. 1, 2)	☐	☐	☐
Describe towns and cities (Ex. 2)	☐	☐	☐
Ask for and make suggestions (Ex. 2, 3, 4)	☐	☐	☐
Ask and answer questions about experiences (Ex. 3, 4)	☐	☐	☐
Ask for and give advice about problems (Ex. 4)	☐	☐	☐

1 LISTENING So, you're from Hawaii?

▶ **A** Listen to Megan talk about Honolulu. What does she say about these things?
Complete the chart.

1. size of city _____	**3.** prices of things _____
2. weather _____	**4.** Waikiki Beach _____

B Write sentences comparing Honolulu with your hometown.
Then discuss with a partner.

> Honolulu isn't too big, but Seoul is really big.

2 ROLE PLAY My hometown

Student A: Imagine you are planning to visit Student B's hometown.
Ask questions to learn more about the place. Use the
questions in the box and your own ideas.

Student B: Answer Student A's questions about your hometown.

    A: What's your hometown like?
    B: It's very interesting, but it's crowded and polluted.

Change roles and try the role play again.

possible questions
What's your hometown like?
How big is it?
What's the weather like?
Is it expensive?
What should you see there?
What can you do there?

3 DISCUSSION Medicines and remedies

A GROUP WORK Write your suggestions for these common problems and then discuss your ideas in groups.

a stomachache

an insect bite

the hiccups

a nosebleed

For a stomachache, it's a good idea to . . .

A: What can you do for a stomachache?
B: I think it's helpful to drink herbal tea.
C: Yes. And it's a good idea to see a doctor.

B GROUP WORK What health problems do you visit a doctor for? go to a drugstore for? use a home remedy for? Ask for advice and remedies.

4 SPEAKING What's your advice?

A GROUP WORK Read these people's problems. Suggest advice for each problem. Then choose the best advice.

I'm visiting the United States. I'm staying with a family while I'm here. What small gifts can I get for them?

My co-worker always talks loudly to his friends during work hours. I can't concentrate! What can I do?

Our school wants to buy some new gym equipment. Can you suggest some good ways to raise money?

A: Why doesn't she give them some flowers? They're always nice.
B: That's a good idea. Or she could bring chocolates.
C: I think she should . . .

B CLASS ACTIVITY Share your group's advice for each problem with the class.

WHAT'S NEXT?

Look at your Self-assessment again. Do you need to review anything?

13 What would you like?

▸ Agree and disagree about food preferences
▸ Order food in a restaurant

1 SNAPSHOT

Favorite Foods

apple pie

☐ brought to North America from Europe in the 17th century

chocolate

☐ originally prepared as a drink by the Olmec people in Mexico over 3,000 years ago

french fries

☐ first made in Belgium around 1680

hamburger

☐ created around 1900 in the U.S. as a quick and inexpensive meal

ice-cream cone

☐ created at the 1904 World's Fair in the U.S. by a Syrian chef, Ernest Hamwi

pasta

☐ first written about in a Greek recipe from the 1st century CE

the sandwich

☐ named for the English Earl of Sandwich in the 1760s

sushi

☐ modern style sushi first made in Japan in the 1820s

What are these foods made of? Put the foods in order from your favorite (1) to your least favorite (8).
What are three other foods you enjoy? Which have you eaten recently?

2 CONVERSATION I'm tired of shopping.

▶ **A** Listen and practice.

Simon: Hey, do you want to get something to eat?

Kristin: Sure. I'm tired of shopping.

Simon: So am I. What do you think of Thai food?

Kristin: I love it, but I'm not really in the mood for it today.

Simon: Yeah. I'm not either, I guess. It's a bit spicy.

Kristin: What about Japanese food?

Simon: Fine by me! I love Japanese food.

Kristin: So do I. There's a great restaurant on the first floor. It's called Kyoto Garden.

Simon: Perfect. Let's go try it.

▶ **B** Listen to the rest of the conversation. What do they decide to do after eating? Is there something they don't want to do?

3 GRAMMAR FOCUS

▶ *So, too, neither, either*

	Agree	Disagree
I'm crazy about Italian food.	**So am** I./I **am, too.**	Oh, **I'm not.**
I **can** eat really spicy food.	**So can** I./I **can, too.**	Really? I **can't.**
I **like** Japanese food a lot.	**So do** I./I **do, too.**	Oh, I **don't (like it very much).**
I'm not in the mood for Indian food.	**Neither am** I./**I'm not either.**	Really? I **am.**
I **can't** stand fast food.	**Neither can** I./I **can't either.**	Oh, I **love** it!
I **don't like** salty food.	**Neither do** I./I **don't either.**	Oh, I **like** it a lot.

GRAMMAR PLUS *see page 144*

bland

delicious

greasy

healthy

rich

salty

spicy

A Write responses to show agreement with these statements.
Then compare with a partner.

1. I'm not crazy about Italian food. _____
2. I can eat any kind of food. _____
3. I think Indian food is delicious. _____
4. I can't stand greasy food. _____
5. I don't like salty food. _____
6. I'm in the mood for something spicy. _____
7. I'm tired of fast food. _____
8. I don't enjoy rich food very much. _____
9. I always eat healthy food. _____
10. I can't eat bland food. _____

B **PAIR WORK** Take turns responding to the statements in part A again.
Give your own opinion when responding.

C Write statements about these things. (You will use the statements in Exercise 4.)

1. two kinds of food you like
2. two kinds of food you can't stand
3. two kinds of food you would like to eat today

4 PRONUNCIATION Stress in responses

▶ **A** Listen and practice. Notice how the last word of each response is stressed.

●　　　　　　●　　　　　　●　　　　　　●

I do, too.	So do I.	I don't either.	Neither do I.
I am, too.	So am I.	I'm not either.	Neither am I.
I can, too.	So can I.	I can't either.	Neither can I.

B PAIR WORK Read and respond to the statements your partner wrote
for Exercise 3, part C. Pay attention to the stress in your responses.

5 WORD POWER Food categories

A Complete the chart. Then add one more word to each category.

bread	fish	mangoes	peas	shrimp
chicken	grapes	octopus	potatoes	strawberries
corn	lamb	pasta	rice	turkey

Fruit	Vegetables	Grains	Meat	Seafood

B GROUP WORK What's your favorite food in each category?
Are there any you haven't tried?

6 CONVERSATION May I take your order?

Today's Specials

soup of the day
chicken curry and mango salad
veggie burger with soup or salad
red bean chili and chips

▶ **A** Listen and practice.

Server May I take your order?

Customer Yes, please. I'd like the veggie burger.

Server All right. And would you like soup
or salad with your burger?

Customer What's the soup of the day?

Server It's chicken soup. We also have cream
of potato soup and onion soup.

Customer I'll have the onion soup, please.

Server And would you like anything to drink?

Customer Yes, I'd like a lemonade, please.

▶ **B** Listen to the server talk to the next customer.
What does he order?

7 GRAMMAR FOCUS

Modal verbs *would* and *will* for requests

		Contractions
What **would** you **like**?	I**'d like** the veggie burger.	
	I**'ll have** a mango salad.	I**'ll** = I will
What kind of soup **would** you **like**?	I**'d like** onion soup, please.	I**'d** = I would
	I**'ll have** the soup of the day.	
What **would** you **like** to drink?	I**'d like** a lemonade.	
	I**'ll have** a large orange juice.	
Would you **like** anything else?	Yes, please. I**'d like** some coffee.	
	That's all, thanks.	

GRAMMAR PLUS *see page 144*

Complete this conversation. Then practice with a partner.

Server: What _____ you like to order?

Customer: I _____ have the spicy fish.

Server: _____ you like salad or potatoes?

Customer: I _____ like potatoes, please.

Server: OK. And _____ you like anything to drink?

Customer: I _____ just have a glass of water.

Server: Would you _____ anything else?

Customer: No, that's all for now, thanks.

Later

Server: Would you _____ dessert?

Customer: Yes, I _____ like ice cream.

Server: What flavor _____ you like?

Customer: Hmm. I _____ have mint chocolate chip, please.

8 ROLE PLAY At a coffee shop

Student A: You are a customer at a coffee shop. Order what you want for lunch.

Student B: You are the server. Take your customer's order.

TODAY'S LUNCH SPECIALS

Cheeseburger with onion rings

Spicy shrimp and rice

Chicken salad sandwich

Lamb curry and potatoes

Sushi plate with miso soup

Vegetarian pizza and salad

Drinks

Coffee   Fresh juice

Tea   Sparkling water

Soda

Desserts

Ice cream   Lemon pie

Chocolate cake   Fresh fruit salad

Change roles and try the role play again.

LISTENING Working late

▶ **A** Steven and Sarah are working late. Listen as their boss asks what they would like for dinner. What do they order? Fill in their choices.

Steven	Sarah
_____ pizza	_____ pizza
Salad with _____	Salad with _____ dressing
Drink: _____ with	Drink: _____ with
_____	_____
Dessert: a piece of _____	Dessert: a slice of _____

▶ **B** Listen to their conversation after the food arrives. Choose the two items that are missing from the order.

10 **INTERCHANGE 13** Planning a food festival

Create a menu to offer at a food festival. Go to Interchange 13 on page 128.

11 **WRITING** A restaurant review

A Have you eaten out recently? Write a review of a restaurant, café, or food truck. Choose at least five questions from the list. Answer these questions and add ideas of your own.

What's the name of the place?
When did you go there?
What time did you go?
Who did you go with?
What did you have to eat?
What did you have to drink?
Did you order dessert?
What did you like about the place?
What didn't you like about it?
Would you recommend it? Why?
  Why not?

B **GROUP WORK** Take turns reading your reviews. Which place would you like to try?

USER REVIEW

Last Saturday, my sister and I tried Burger To Go, a new restaurant in our town. I had a classic cheeseburger and fries. The burger wasn't very big, but it was delicious. The fries were hot and crispy but a little too salty. For dessert, I had apple pie. It wasn't bad, but I've had better. I would recommend Burger To Go for their burgers and their very friendly service. I hope they improve with time!
– Emilia

A Scan the article. In which country do people usually leave a 15–20% tip on food? In which country is tipping unnecessary?

TO TIP OR NOT TO TIP?

WHAT'S A TIP?

The verb *to tip* means to give money, and the noun *tip* is the money that you give to someone. It's a slang word from Old English. Around the world, many people give tips to people who provide a service for them. It's a way of saying thank you. But did you know that tipping customs around the world *vary* a lot?

WHO AND WHERE TO TIP

In some countries, like the United States, it's common to give a tip in a lot of different places. Almost everybody gives tips to servers in restaurants and cafés. Servers *rely on* those tips to add to the low *wages* they get paid for their jobs. People also tip taxi drivers and hairstylists. If an airport worker or a hotel bellhop helps you with a heavy suitcase, you tip them as well. In Japan, though, it's a very different story. In Japan, tipping isn't part of the culture, so it rarely happens. In fact, a tip might be *confusing* to the server. And in France, a "service charge" is included on all restaurant checks, so in fact, you've already tipped your server.

HOW MUCH TO TIP?

The amount people tip in the United States varies between 15 and 20% on restaurant checks. So, for example, if a restaurant total is $40, people give the server around $6–8. That seems like a lot of money for some visitors who come from countries where tipping isn't *customary*. According to one news source, the average tip in a New York restaurant is 19.1% of the total, but in London it's 11.8%. That's a big difference.

WHO'S THE BEST TIPPER?

A millionaire named Benjamin Olewine probably wins the prize for giving the world's most *generous* tip. Mr. Olewine paid for his server's nursing school fees as a tip! The waitress, Melissa, was working in a restaurant to save money for school. One day, she served breakfast to Mr. Olewine. The check was $3.45. The tip was more than $20,000!

B Read the article. Find the words in italics, then check (✓) the correct meaning of each word.

1. *vary*
- ☐ change
- ☐ stay the same

2. *rely on*
- ☐ ask for
- ☐ need

3. *wages*
- ☐ regular pay for a job
- ☐ tips received for a job

4. *confusing*
- ☐ unnecessary
- ☐ difficult to understand

5. *customary*
- ☐ usual
- ☐ unusual

6. *generous*
- ☐ very rich
- ☐ giving more than enough

C Check (✓) the statements that describe correct tipping behavior. For the items you don't check, what is acceptable?

- ☐ **1.** You're eating at a restaurant in London. You leave a 25% tip.
- ☐ **2.** You give your New York server a 15% tip.
- ☐ **3.** You give a large tip after your meal in Tokyo.
- ☐ **4.** Your bellhop in Chicago helps you carry your suitcase. You give him a tip.
- ☐ **5.** You pay your check in Paris and don't leave a tip.

D GROUP WORK Is tipping customary in your country? If it is, who do you tip and how much? If it isn't, what do you think about tipping?

14 It's the coldest city!

▶ Describe and compare different places in the world
▶ Describe temperatures, distances, and measurements

1 WORD POWER Places around the world

A Match the words from the list to the letters in the picture. Then compare with a partner.

1. beach _____
2. desert _____
3. forest _____
4. hill _____
5. island _____
6. lake _____
7. mountain _____
8. ocean _____
9. river _____
10. valley _____
11. volcano _____
12. waterfall _____

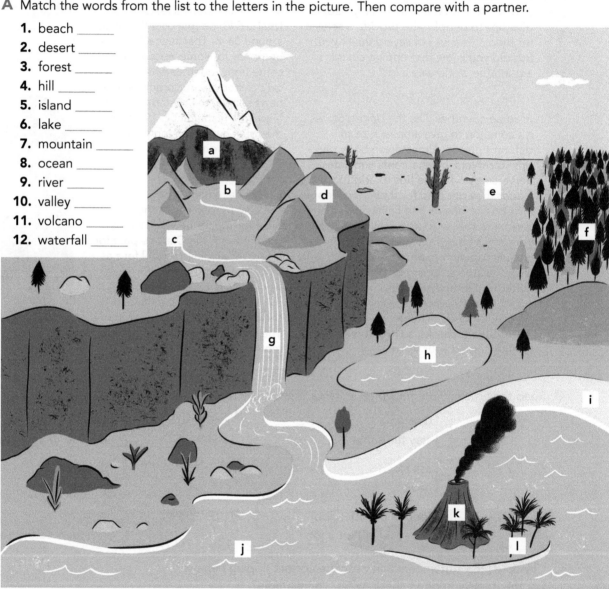

B **PAIR WORK** What other geography words can you think of? Do you see any of these places in the picture above?

C **GROUP WORK** Try to think of famous examples for each item in part A.

A: A famous beach is Shirahama Beach in Japan.

B: And the Sahara is a famous . . .

2 CONVERSATION I love quizzes!

A Listen and practice.

Claire: This is one of the best airline magazines I've ever read. Oh, look! A quiz! "Our world – How much do you know?"

Steve: Oh, I love quizzes! Ask me the questions.

Claire: Sure. First question: Which country is larger, Mexico or Australia?

Steve: I know. Australia is larger than Mexico.

Claire: OK, next. What's the longest river in the world?

Steve: That's easy. It's the Nile!

Claire: All right. Here's a hard one. Which country is more crowded, Malta or England?

Steve: I'm not sure. I think Malta is more crowded.

Claire: Really? OK, one more. Which city is the most expensive: Hong Kong, London, or Paris?

Steve: Oh, that's easy. Paris is the most expensive.

B Listen to the rest of the conversation. How many questions did Steve get right?

3 GRAMMAR FOCUS

Comparisons with adjectives

Which country is **larger**, Australia or Mexico?
  Australia is **larger than** Mexico.

Which country is **the largest** in the world?
  Russia is **the largest** country.

Which is **more crowded**? Malta or England?
  Malta is **more crowded than** England.
  Malta is **the most crowded** country in Europe.

Adjective	Comparative	Superlative
long	longer	the longest
large	larger	the largest
dry	drier	the driest
big	bigger	the biggest
beautiful	more beautiful	the most beautiful
crowded	more crowded	the most crowded
expensive	more expensive	the most expensive
good	better	the best
bad	worse	the worst

GRAMMAR PLUS see page 145

A Complete questions 1 to 4 with comparatives and questions 5 to 8 with superlatives. Then ask and answer the questions.

1. Which country is _____, Monaco or Vatican City? (small)
2. Which waterfall is _____, Niagara Falls or Victoria Falls? (high)
3. Which city is _____, Hong Kong or Cairo? (crowded)
4. Which lake is _____, Lake Michigan or Lake Baikal? (large)
5. Which is _____: Mount Aconcagua, Mount Everest, or Mount Fuji? (high)
6. What is _____ river in the Americas, the Mississippi, the Colorado, or the Amazon? (long)
7. Which city is _____: London, Tokyo, or Moscow? (expensive)
8. What is _____ ocean in the world, the Pacific, the Atlantic, or the Arctic? (deep)

B CLASS ACTIVITY Write four questions like those in part A about your country or other countries. Then ask your classmates the questions.

4 PRONUNCIATION Questions of choice

▶ **A** Listen and practice. Notice how the intonation in questions of choice drops, then rises, and then drops again.

Which city is more crowded, Hong Kong or Cairo?

Which city is the most expensive: London, Tokyo, or Moscow?

B **PAIR WORK** Take turns asking these questions. Pay attention to your intonation. Do you know the answers?

Which desert is bigger, the Gobi or the Atacama?

Which city is higher, Bogotá or La Paz?

Which ocean is the smallest: the Arctic, the Indian, or the Atlantic?

Which mountains are the highest: the Andes, the Rockies, or the Himalayas?

5 SPEAKING Travelers' tips

GROUP WORK Imagine these people are planning to visit your country. What would they enjoy doing? Agree on a recommendation for each person.

Jana

" I like all kinds of outdoor activities, especially hiking and bike riding. I can't stand crowded and polluted cities."

Neil

" I enjoy visiting museums, trying local food, and shopping at small stores. I don't like boring tourist places."

Sammie

" I love nightlife. My favorite activity is going dancing and meeting new people! I really don't like small towns."

6 LISTENING Quiz Show!

▶ Listen to three people on a TV quiz show. Check (✓) the correct answers.

1.	☐ the Eiffel Tower	☐ the Statue of Liberty	☐ the Panama Canal
2.	☐ Victoria Falls	☐ Niagara Falls	☐ Angel Falls
3.	☐ gold	☐ butter	☐ all
4.	☐ the Arctic Ocean	☐ the Southern Ocean	☐ the Indian Ocean
5.	☐ São Paulo	☐ Mexico City	☐ Seoul
6.	☐ Africa	☐ Antarctica	☐ Australia

You probably know more than you think! Take a quiz. Go to Interchange 14 on page 129.

8 SNAPSHOT

8 Surprising Facts

1 The hottest place in the world is Death Valley, California. The temperature there has reached 134°F (56.7°C).

2 Antarctica is the largest desert on Earth. It is 5.4 million square miles (14 million square kilometers). It's also the coldest, windiest continent.

3 *NCIS* is the world's most watched TV show. Over 55 million people across the world have watched it.

4 The largest cat in the world is the Siberian tiger. At 700 pounds (320 kilos), it is bigger than a lion.

5 France is the most popular country to visit. It gets over 80 million visitors a year.

6 The highest price for a car at an auction was just over $38 million for a 1962 Ferrari. The auction happened in 2014.

7 The best-selling music album of all time is Michael Jackson's *Thriller*. The 1982 album has sold around 65 million copies.

8 The planet in our Solar System with the most moons, 67 total, is Jupiter. The largest one, Ganymede, is the ninth largest object in the Solar System.

Which facts do you find surprising? Why?

What are some facts about your country? What's the tallest building?
 the busiest airport? the most popular city to visit?

9 CONVERSATION That's freezing!

▶ **A** Listen and practice.

Alberto: Hi, Lily. You're from Canada, right? I'm going to Toronto in January.

Lily: Actually, I'm from the U.S., but I went to school in Toronto. Winter there can be pretty cold.

Alberto: How cold is it on average?

Lily: Um, I think the average in January is around 20° or maybe 25°.

Alberto: Twenty-five degrees? But that's warm!

Lily: Twenty-five degrees Fahrenheit. That's about . . . minus 3 or 4 Celsius.

Alberto: Minus 3 or 4? That's freezing!

Lily: Oh, come on, that's not *so* cold, at least not where I'm from.

Alberto: Really? Where are you from?

Lily: Well, I live in Fairbanks, Alaska, around 3,000 miles from Toronto. That's . . . let me check on my phone . . . Yes, that's about 4,800 kilometers.

Alberto: Wow. . . . So, is it colder than Toronto?

Lily: It's much colder than Toronto. It's the coldest city in the United States!

▶ **B** Listen to the rest of the conversation. Is Fairbanks a small town? What else does Lily say about it?

10 GRAMMAR FOCUS

▶ **Questions with *how***

How cold is Toronto in the winter?	It gets down to minus 25° Celsius.	(-13° Fahrenheit)
How hot is Fairbanks in the summer?	It gets up to about 20° Celsius.	(68° Fahrenheit)
How far is Toronto from Fairbanks?	It's about 4,800 kilometers.	(3,000 miles)
How big is Seoul?	It's 605 square kilometers.	(233.6 square miles)
How high is Mount Everest?	It's 8,848 meters **high**.	(29,028 feet)
How long is the Mississippi River?	It's about 3,700 kilometers **long**.	(2,300 miles)
How deep is the Grand Canyon?	It's about 1,828 meters **deep**.	(6,000 feet)

GRAMMAR PLUS *see page 145*

A Write the questions to these answers. Then practice with a partner.

1. **A:** _____?
   B: Niagara Falls is 52 meters (170 feet) high.

2. **A:** _____?
   B: California is about 423,970 square kilometers (163,670 square miles).

3. **A:** _____?
   B: The Nile is 6,670 kilometers (4,145 miles) long.

4. **A:** _____?
   B: Osaka is about 400 kilometers (250 miles) from Tokyo.

5. **A:** _____?
   B: Mexico City gets up to about 28° Celsius (82° Fahrenheit) in the summer.

B **GROUP WORK** Think of five questions with *how* about places in your country or other countries you know. Ask and answer your questions.

11 WRITING An article about a place

A Write an article about a place in your country or in another country that you think tourists would like to visit. Describe a place from the list.

- a beach
- a desert
- an island
- a lake
- a mountain
- a river
- a volcano
- a waterfall

B **PAIR WORK** Read your partner's article. Ask questions to get more information.

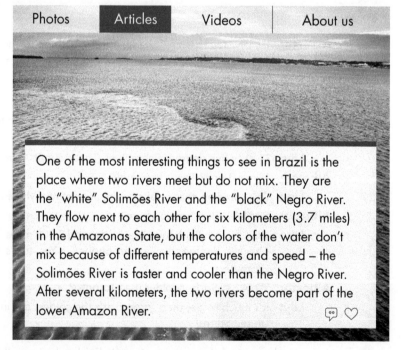

| Photos | Articles | Videos | About us |

One of the most interesting things to see in Brazil is the place where two rivers meet but do not mix. They are the "white" Solimões River and the "black" Negro River. They flow next to each other for six kilometers (3.7 miles) in the Amazonas State, but the colors of the water don't mix because of different temperatures and speed – the Solimões River is faster and cooler than the Negro River. After several kilometers, the two rivers become part of the lower Amazon River.

A Look at the title of the article and the pictures. Why do you think these places are so clean?

Earth's Cleanest Places

Lake Vostok, Antarctica

About four kilometers (2.5 miles) under a large area of ice in Antarctica, there's a lake named Lake Vostok. It covers 15,690 square kilometers (6,058 square miles) and is 800 meters (2,625 feet) deep in some places. Lake Vostok is prehistoric – millions of years old – but until 1956, no one even knew it existed. It's a fresh water lake, and it has been hidden from sunlight for 15 million years. What this means is that the water is some of the cleanest, purest water on Earth.

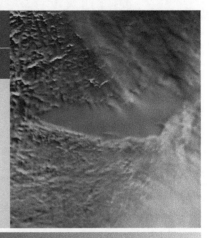

Cape Grim, Australia

We all know that air pollution is a problem all around the world, so where do you go if you want really clean air? Well, Cape Grim in Tasmania, Australia is probably the best idea. Cape Grim has some of the cleanest air on Earth. Cape Grim also has beautiful, clean water. Why is this? Wind! Special winds called "The Roaring Forties" cross the Southern Ocean, bringing with them wonderfully clean water and air. In fact, in Cape Grim, people are allowed to put rain water into bottles and sell it. That's how clean it is!

Singapore

The tiny island of Singapore has a population of about 5.7 million people. It also has very strict rules about the way its people behave. Singapore is one of the cleanest cities on the planet because of these rules. People are not allowed to chew gum unless it's from a doctor, and all used chewing gum has to go in a trash can. That means that you don't find gum on the sidewalks. In fact, no one drops trash in the street. There are big fines for people who don't respect the rules, but most people are happy to keep their city clean and healthy.

B Read the article. What is the main goal of the article? Check (✓) the correct answer.

☐ to entertain people ☐ to inform people ☐ to persuade people to do something

C Read the article and answer the questions.

1. When did people discover Lake Vostok? _____

2. How long has Lake Vostok been hidden? _____

3. What two things is Cape Grim famous for? _____

4. What's the main reason that Cape Grim is so clean? _____

5. About how many people live in Singapore? _____

6. What happens when people break the rules in Singapore? _____

D **GROUP WORK** What do you think is the cleanest place in your country? Why is it so clean? How would you describe it to a friend?

SELF-ASSESSMENT

How well can you do these things? Check (✓) the boxes.

I can . . .	Very well	OK	A little
Say what I like and dislike (Ex. 1)	☐	☐	☐
Agree and disagree with other people (Ex. 1)	☐	☐	☐
Understand a variety of questions in a restaurant (Ex. 2)	☐	☐	☐
Order a meal in a restaurant (Ex. 3)	☐	☐	☐
Describe and compare things, people, and places (Ex. 4, 5)	☐	☐	☐
Ask questions about distances and measurements (Ex. 5)	☐	☐	☐

1 SPEAKING Survey: food preferences

A Answer these questions. Write your responses under the column "My answers."
Then add one more question to the chart.

	My answers	Classmate's name
What food are you crazy about?		
What food can't you stand?		
Do you like vegetarian food?		
Can you eat very spicy food?		
How often do you go out to eat?		
What restaurant do you like a lot?		

B CLASS ACTIVITY Go around the class. Find someone who has the same opinions or habits.

A: I'm crazy about Japanese food.
B: I am, too./So am I. OR Oh, I'm not. I'm crazy about . . .

2 LISTENING In a restaurant

Listen to six requests in a restaurant. Check (✓) the best response.

1. ☐ Yes. This way, please.
☐ Yes, please.

2. ☐ No, I don't.
☐ Yes, I'll have tea, please.

3. ☐ I'd like the fish, please.
☐ Yes, I would.

4. ☐ I'll have a green salad.
☐ Italian, please.

5. ☐ Broccoli, please.
☐ Yes, I would.

6. ☐ Yes, I'd like more water.
☐ No, I don't think so.

3 ROLE PLAY May I take your order?

Student A: Imagine you are a server and Student B is a customer. Take his or her order and write it on the check.

Student B: Imagine you are a hungry customer at any restaurant you choose. Student A is a server. Order a meal.

Change roles and try the role play again.

THANK YOU   TOTAL: ....

4 SPEAKING Your hometown quiz

A PAIR WORK Write down six facts about your town or city using comparatives or superlatives. Then write six Wh-questions based on your facts.

> 1. The longest street is Independence Street.
>
> What's the longest street in our city?

B GROUP WORK Join another pair. Take turns asking the other pair your questions. How many can they answer correctly?

5 GAME What's the question?

A Think of three statements that can be answered with *how* questions or Wh-questions with comparatives and superlatives. Write each statement on a separate card.

B CLASS ACTIVITY Divide into Teams A and B. Shuffle the cards together. One student from Team A picks a card and reads it to a student from Team B. That student tries to make a question for it.

A: The Atacama is drier than the Sahara.
B: Which desert is drier, the Atacama or the Sahara?

Keep score. The team with the most correct questions wins.

> June and July are the coldest months in our city.

> The Atacama is drier than the Sahara.

> It's about two kilometers from my house to the school.

WHAT'S NEXT?

Look at your Self-assessment again. Do you need to review anything?

15 What are you doing later?

▶ Discuss future activities and plans
▶ Give messages

1 SNAPSHOT

HOW TO DECLINE AN INVITATION POLITELY

A friend has invited you to go out, but you can't make it.
Follow our advice and learn how you can decline an
invitation politely and keep your friend.

To thank your friend, you can say:
"Thanks so much for asking me. It sounds like a lot of fun."
"Thanks so much for the invite."

To apologize and explain why you can't accept, you can say:
"Sorry, but I already have plans."
"Sorry, but I have something else going on that day."
"I'm so sorry, but I can't make it. I'm really busy these days."

To offer another time to do something together, you can say:
"This week is crazy, but let's shoot for next week."
"Maybe another time? I'm free next week."
"Can I take a rain check?"

Do you feel comfortable declining friends' invitations? Why? Why not?
What polite excuses have you used? Which are effective? Which are not?
What is the best tip, in your opinion? Why?

2 CONVERSATION Are you doing anything tomorrow?

▶ **A** Listen and practice.

Alicia: Hey, Mike, what are you doing tonight? Do
you want to go see the new photo exhibit?

Mike: Thanks so much for asking me, but I can't.
I'm going to have dinner with my parents.

Alicia: Oh, well, maybe some other time.

Mike: Are you doing anything tomorrow?
We could go then.

Alicia: Tomorrow sounds fine. I have class until four.

Mike: So let's go around five.

Alicia: OK. Afterward, maybe we can get some dinner.

Mike: Sounds great.

▶ **B** Listen to the rest of the conversation. Where are
Alicia and Mike going to have dinner? Who are they
going to meet for dinner?

3 GRAMMAR FOCUS

▶ **Future with present continuous and *be going to***

With present continuous	With *be going to* + verb	Time expressions
What **are** you **doing** tonight?	What **is** she **going to do** tomorrow?	tonight
I**'m going** to a party.	She**'s going to see a play.**	tomorrow
Are you **doing** anything tomorrow?	**Are** they **going to see** the photo exhibit?	on Friday
No, I**'m** not (**doing** anything).	Yes, they **are** (**going to see** it).	this weekend
		next week

GRAMMAR PLUS *see page 146*

A Complete the invitations in column A with the present continuous used as future.
Complete the responses in column B with *be going to*.

A

1. What _____ you _____ (do) tonight? Would you like to go out?

2. _____ you _____ (do) anything on Friday night? Do you want to see a movie?

3. We _____ (have) friends over for a barbecue on Sunday. Would you and your parents like to come?

4. _____ you _____ (stay) in town next weekend? Do you want to go for a hike?

B

a. I _____ (be) here on Saturday, but not Sunday. Let's try to go on Saturday.

b. Well, my father _____ (visit) my brother at college. But my mother and I _____ (be) home. We'd love to come!

c. Sorry, I can't. I _____ (work) late tonight. How about tomorrow night?

d. Can we go to a late show? I _____ (stay) at the office till 7:00.

B Match the invitations in column A with the responses in column B.
Then practice with a partner.

4 WORD POWER Free-time activities and events

A Complete the chart with words and phrases from the list.
Then add one more example to each category.

a rock concert	a barbecue	a wedding	a hip-hop dance performance
a soccer game	a film festival	a musical	a video game tournament
a birthday party	a class reunion	a car race	a baseball game

Sports and games	Friends and family	Art and performances

B PAIR WORK Are you going to do any of the activities in part A?
When are you doing them? Talk with a partner.

5 ROLE PLAY Accept or refuse?

Student A: Choose an activity from Exercise 4 and invite a partner to go with you. Be ready to say where and when the activity is.

> **A:** So, are you doing anything on . . . ? Would you like to . . . ?

Student B: Your partner invites you out. Either accept the invitation and ask for more information or say you can't go and give an excuse.

Accept	**Refuse**
B: OK. That sounds fun. Where is it?	**B:** Oh, I'm sorry, I can't. I'm . . .

Change roles and try the role play again.

6 INTERCHANGE 15 Weekend plans

Find out what your classmates are going to do this weekend. Go to Interchange 15 on page 130.

7 CONVERSATION Can I take a message?

▶ **A** Listen and practice.

CAITLIN Hello?

JAKE Hi, Caitlin. It's Jake. Are you busy?

CAITLIN No, I'm having coffee with Brittney. Where are you? Class is going to start soon.

JAKE That's the problem. I don't think I'm going to make it tonight.

CAITLIN Why not? What's the matter?

JAKE My bus is stuck in traffic. Nobody is moving.

CAITLIN Oh, no! What are you going to do?

JAKE I don't know. Could you tell Mr. Eaton that I'm going to miss class?

CAITLIN No problem. I'll give him the message.

JAKE Oh, and could you ask Brittney to take pictures of the whiteboard for me?

CAITLIN Sure. But I can take the pictures.

JAKE Um, thanks, but the last time you took a picture of the board all I could see was the wall!

▶ **B** Listen to three other phone calls. Write the callers' names.

8 GRAMMAR FOCUS

▶ **Formal and informal messages with *tell* and *ask***

Statements	Messages with a statement: *tell*	
I'm going to miss class tonight.	(Please) **Tell him (that)** I'm going to miss class.	informal ↓ formal
	Could you tell him (that) I'm going to miss class?	
	Would you tell him (that) I'm going to miss class?	
Requests	**Messages with a request: *ask***	
Could she take a picture of the board?	(Please) **Ask her** to take a picture of the board.	informal ↓ formal
	Could you ask her to take a picture of the board?	
	Would you ask her to take a picture of the board?	

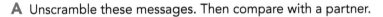

GRAMMAR PLUS *see page 146*

A Unscramble these messages. Then compare with a partner.

1. tell / that / is / please / Haru / the barbecue / on Saturday

_____.

2. call me / at / 4:00 / you / Caitlin / could /ask / to

_____?

3. is / that / Mia / tonight / could / you / the dance performance / tell

_____?

4. tell / is / Casey / in the park / would / you / that / the picnic

_____?

5. meet me / to / you / would / Maika / ask / at the stadium

_____?

6. ask / to the rock concert / please / bring / Garrett / to / the tickets

_____.

B **PAIR WORK** Imagine that you are far from school and cannot come to class. "Call" your partner and ask him or her to give a message to your teacher and to one of the students in your group.

A: Could you tell Ms. Clark that . . . And could you ask Joel to . . .

9 WRITING Text message requests

A **PAIR WORK** "Text" your partner. Write messages to each other with requests for your classmates. Write as many messages as you can in three minutes.

> A: Hi, Sandra. Would you ask Marcella to have
> dinner with us after class?
> B: OK, Chris. And could you tell Jules that we have
> a test tomorrow?

B **CLASS ACTIVITY** Give the messages to your classmates.

A: Hi, Jules. I have a message from Sandra.
We have a test tomorrow.
B: Hi, Marcella. I have a message from Chris.
Would you like to have dinner with us after class?

10 PRONUNCIATION Reduction of *could you* and *would you*

▶ **A** Listen and practice. Notice how **could you** and **would you** are reduced in conversation.

[cʊdʒə]
Could you tell him I'm going to miss class?

[wʊdʒə]
Would you ask him to call me after class?

B PAIR WORK Practice these questions with reduced forms.

Could you tell them I'm in bed with a cold?

Would you ask her to be on time?

Could you ask her to return my dictionary?

Would you tell him there's a food festival tomorrow?

11 LISTENING I'm going to be late.

▶ Listen to four people leaving messages. Who is the message from?
Who is it for? What is the message? Complete the chart.

1
Message from: _____
Message for: _____
Message: _____
_____

2
Message from: _____
Message for: _____
Message: _____
_____

3
Message from: _____
Message for: _____
Message: _____
_____

4
Message from: _____
Message for: _____
Message: _____
_____

12 ROLE PLAY Who's calling?

Student A: You have a computer repair store. A client, Sophie Green, has left her laptop at your store. Call her to tell her this:

The computer needs a new motherboard. It's going to cost $250.
She can buy a used motherboard for $90. Could she please call you before 5:00?

Student B: Someone calls for your mother, Sophie Green. She isn't at home. Take a message for her.

Change roles and try another role play.

Student A: You are a receptionist at Techniware Industries. Someone calls for your boss, Mr. Yun. He isn't in. Take a message for him.

Student B: Call Mr. Yun at Techniware Industries to tell him this:

You can't make your lunch meeting at 12:00 next Wednesday. You would like to meet at 12:30 at the same place instead. Could he please call you to arrange the new time?

> **useful expressions**
>
> **Caller**
> May I speak to . . . ?
> Can I leave a message?
>
> **Receiver**
> Sorry, but . . . isn't here.
> Can I take a message?
> I'll give him/her the message.

13 READING

A Scan the article. Why did some people go to the wrong address?

Home	News	Technology	Lifestyle	Fashion	Politics	Food		Q

Cell Phone Trouble!

Have you ever had an embarrassing time because of your cell phone? If you have, you're not alone. Check out this selection of cell phone "accidents."

Security cameras in a fancy hotel captured a video of a well-dressed woman, about 30 years old, texting on her phone. There's nothing unusual about that, is there? Well, yes, this time there is. The woman was so busy on her phone that she walked right into a pool of water in the hotel lobby . . . fully dressed! Nobody knows who the woman is or where the watery adventure happened, but almost half a million people have watched the video on the Internet!

A New Yorker was riding the subway home from work one evening. He was very excited by the video game he was playing on his smartphone. When he won the game, he threw his arms in the air in excitement . . . At that moment, the subway doors opened to let people on and off the train. The problem is that the man threw his phone right out of the subway car and on to the tracks below. Oops! No more video games for a while!

A lot of people are so busy looking at their smartphones that they often walk into lampposts and hurt themselves. The problem is so big that Brick Lane in London is now a "safe text" zone. Every lamppost in the street is covered in soft padding just in case somebody walks into it.

Most of us use map apps on our phones to get to the places we want to go. But sometimes, these apps get a little confused. A demolition company (a company that tears down buildings) used a map app to find a house. So far so good, right? Well, no. The map led the workers to the wrong house, a house one block away from the correct house in a town in Texas. The workers tore the house down. Imagine the owner's reaction when she arrived back home later that day!

B Read the article. Which advice best summarizes the article?

1. London is a great place to visit if you like using cell phones.
2. Be careful when you use your cell phone.
3. Lampposts and water are extremely dangerous.

C Check the facts that are mentioned in the article.

- [ ] **1.** A woman on a subway fell into some water while she was using her phone.
- [ ] **2.** Many people have watched a video of a woman falling into water.
- [ ] **3.** A man on a subway lost his phone.
- [ ] **4.** The man on the subway didn't like the video game he was playing.
- [ ] **5.** London has an area where you can text more safely.
- [ ] **6.** Every lamppost in London is padded.
- [ ] **7.** A demolition company tore down someone's home.
- [ ] **8.** The torn down building was in Texas.

D **PAIR WORK** Have you ever had a cell phone "accident?" What happened?
What advice about cell phone safety would you give to a child?

16 How have you changed?

- ▶ Describe life changes
- ▶ Describe plans for the future

1 SNAPSHOT

LIFE-CHANGING EXPERIENCES

Change schools	Graduate from college	Fall in love
Move to a new house	Get a job	Get married
Turn 18	Move to a new city	Have children
Get a driver's license	Travel abroad	Retire

Which of these events are the most important changes? Why?
What changes have you gone through in the last year? Which do you expect to happen soon?
What other things bring about change in our lives?

2 CONVERSATION I haven't seen you in ages.

▶ **A** Listen and practice.

Hayden — Hey, Thomas! I haven't seen you since you changed schools! How have you been?

Thomas — Not bad. How about you? Have you finished college?

Hayden — Yeah. I majored in business administration, and I've just started a new job. How about you? Are you still in college?

Thomas — Oh, no, I finished school. I majored in drama. Actually, I'm in a play right now.

Hayden — No kidding! What's the name of the play? I'd love to see it!

Thomas — I'm acting in *A Change for the Better* at the Atlas Theater.

Hayden — Cool! You know, you look different. Have you changed your hair?

Thomas — Yeah, it's longer now. My character has long hair. And I wear contacts.

Hayden — Well, you look fantastic!

Thomas — Thanks, so do you!

▶ **B** Listen to the rest of the conversation. What are some other changes in Hayden's life?

3 GRAMMAR FOCUS

▶ Describing changes

With the present tense
I**'m not** in school anymore.
I **wear** contacts now.

With the past tense
I **majored** in business administration.
I **got** engaged.

With the present perfect
I**'ve** just **started** a new job.
I**'ve bought** a new apartment.

With the comparative
It's **less noisy** than downtown.
My hair is **longer** now.

GRAMMAR PLUS *see page 147*

A How have you changed in the last five years? Check (✓) the statements that are true for you. If a statement isn't true, give the correct information.

- [ ] **1.** I dress differently now.
- [ ] **2.** I've changed my hairstyle.
- [ ] **3.** I've made some new friends.
- [ ] **4.** I got a pet.
- [ ] **5.** I've joined a gym.
- [ ] **6.** I moved into my own apartment.
- [ ] **7.** I'm more outgoing than before.
- [ ] **8.** I'm not in high school anymore.
- [ ] **9.** My life is easier now.
- [ ] **10.** I got married.

B **PAIR WORK** Compare your responses in part A. Have you changed in similar ways?

C **GROUP WORK** Write five sentences describing other changes in your life. Then compare in groups. Who in the group has changed the most?

4 LISTENING Online photo albums

▶ Madison and Zachary are looking through online photo albums. Listen to their conversation. How have they changed? Write down three changes.

Changes

5 WORD POWER Changes

A Complete the word map with phrases from the list. Then add two more examples to each category.

dye my hair
get a bank loan
get a credit card
get a pay raise
grow a beard
improve my English vocabulary
learn a new sport
learn how to dance
open a savings account
pierce my ears
start a new online course
wear contact lenses

APPEARANCE
_____
_____
_____
_____
_____
_____

MONEY
_____
_____
_____
_____
_____

CHANGES

SKILLS
_____
_____
_____
_____
_____
_____

B **PAIR WORK** Have you changed in any of these areas? Tell your partner about a change in each category.

A: I started an Italian cooking class last month. I've always loved Italian food.

B: I've improved my English vocabulary a lot. I always watch movies with English subtitles now.

6 CONVERSATION Planning your future

A Listen and practice.

Matt: So, what are you going to do this year? Any New Year's resolutions?

Robin: Well, I'd love to learn how to play the guitar, so I plan to take lessons.

Matt: That sounds great. I don't have any musical talents, but I'd like to learn how to dance. Maybe I can learn to salsa!

Robin: Why not? I hope to learn to play some Latin music, too.

Matt: I know! We can take a trip to Puerto Rico and spend a month learning guitar and dancing. How about that?

Robin: Uh . . . Matt? I don't have any money. Do you?

Matt: I don't either, but I hope to get a new job soon.

Robin: Have you started looking?

Matt: Not yet, but I plan to start right after the holidays.

B Listen to the rest of the conversation. What kind of job does Matt want? What other plans does Robin have for the new year?

7 GRAMMAR FOCUS

> ### ▶ Verb + infinitive
>
> What **are** you **going to do** this year?
>
> I'm (not) **going to take** a trip to the Caribbean.   I **hope to get** a new job.
> I (don't) **plan to take** guitar lessons.   I'**d like to travel** around the United States.
> I (don't) **want to learn** to dance.   I'**d love to play** the guitar.
>
> GRAMMAR PLUS *see page 147*

A Complete these statements so that they are true for you. Use verb + infinitive as shown in the grammar box. Then add two more statements of your own.

1. I _____ travel abroad.
2. I _____ live with my parents.
3. I _____ get married.
4. I _____ have a lot of children.
5. I _____ make a lot of money!
6. I _____ become famous.
7. I _____ buy a sports car.
8. I _____ learn another language.
9. _____
10. _____

B PAIR WORK Compare your responses with a partner. How are you the same? How are you different?

C GROUP WORK What are your plans for the future? Take turns asking and answering these questions.

What are you going to do after this English class is over?
Do you plan to study English again next year?
What other languages would you like to learn?
What countries would you like to visit? Why?
Do you want to get a (new) job in a few years?
What other changes do you hope to make in your life? Why?

8 PRONUNCIATION Vowel sounds /oʊ/ and /ʌ/

▶ **A** Many words spelled with *o* are pronounced /oʊ/ or /ʌ/. Listen to the difference and practice.

/oʊ/ = don't   smoke   go   loan   own   hope
/ʌ/ = month   love   some   does   young   touch

▶ **B** Listen to these words. Check (✓) the correct pronunciation.

	both	cold	come	home	honey	money	mother	over
/oʊ/	☐	☐	☐	☐	☐	☐	☐	☐
/ʌ/	☐	☐	☐	☐	☐	☐	☐	☐

9 INTERCHANGE 16 Our possible future

Imagine you could do anything, go anywhere, and meet anybody.
Go to Interchange 16 on page 131.

10 SPEAKING An English course abroad

A GROUP WORK You want to take an English course abroad in an English-speaking country. Groups get special discounts, so your whole group has to agree on a trip. Talk about these details and take notes on your group's decisions.

> 1. Where you'd like to study (choose an English-speaking country and city)
> 2. When you'd like to travel (choose month of the year)
> 3. How long you want to stay there
> 4. Where you'd like to stay (choose one): a family home, a dorm, a hostel, an apartment, a hotel
> 5. Courses you plan to take (choose two): grammar, writing, pronunciation, conversation, business English
> 6. Tourist places you hope to see

A: Where would you like to study?
B: How about Australia?
C: Australia is great, but it's going to be too expensive. I'd love to go to London. I've never been there.
D: When do you want to go? I think May and June are the best months.

B CLASS ACTIVITY Present your ideas to the class. If the whole class agrees on one trip, you can get a bigger discount.

11 WRITING Travel plans

A GROUP WORK Work with the same group from Exercise 10. As a group, write to your teacher about your plans for the class trip abroad.

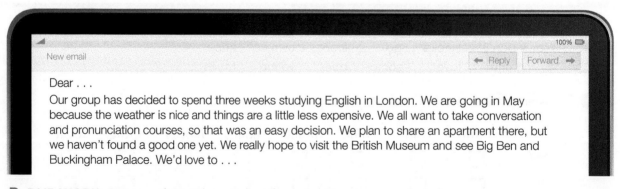

Dear . . .
Our group has decided to spend three weeks studying English in London. We are going in May because the weather is nice and things are a little less expensive. We all want to take conversation and pronunciation courses, so that was an easy decision. We plan to share an apartment there, but we haven't found a good one yet. We really hope to visit the British Museum and see Big Ben and Buckingham Palace. We'd love to . . .

B PAIR WORK Get together with a student from another group and read each other's messages. Do you have similar plans?

A Read the article. What is it about? Check (✓) the correct answer.

☐ Students in the Netherlands ☐ An important invention ☐ Vacations near the ocean

A Goal Accomplished

Boyan Slat has one huge goal. It's a goal that could benefit people and animals all over the world. Amazingly, it looks like he's going to accomplish it.

When he was 16, Dutch engineering student Boyan Slat was on vacation in Greece, and he started to think about all the garbage that gets washed up on beaches. The oceans around the world are full of plastic – millions of tons of plastic. Unfortunately, plastic doesn't just disappear. It takes centuries to break down. Slat wanted to do something to change all that. So he made it a personal goal to clean up the garbage in the world's oceans.

Slat started with an idea for an extraordinary machine to "catch" the plastic floating in the water using the natural energy of the ocean. He left school in 2013 to begin work on his project, which he called The Ocean Cleanup.

A year later, he was leading a team of 100 scientists and engineers working on the invention. Slat needed money for this, so he started asking people to donate to his project online and raised over $2 million!

Soon after, Slat was named a "Champion of the Earth" by the United Nations. It's the most important title the UN gives to people helping the environment. The Ocean Cleanup also won several awards for having one of the best inventions of 2015. But the dream goes on for Boyan Slat. He hopes that the oceans will be free of plastic in about twenty or thirty years.

B Who do you think this article was written for? Choose (✓) the correct answer.

☐ People who care about the environment
☐ College students who want to be inventors
☐ People on vacation who hate garbage

C Read the article and answer the questions.

1. Where was Boyan Slat when he had his big idea?
2. Why did Slat leave school?
3. What is the problem with plastic?
4. How did Slat get the money for his project?
5. When does Slat hope the oceans will be clean?

D **GROUP WORK** Have you had a personal goal that you achieved? Or do you know someone who achieved an amazing personal goal? What was the goal?

SELF-ASSESSMENT

How well can you do these things? Check (✓) the boxes.

I can . . .	Very well	OK	A little
Discuss future plans and arrangements (Ex. 1)	☐	☐	☐
Make and respond to invitations (Ex. 2)	☐	☐	☐
Understand and pass on telephone messages (Ex. 3)	☐	☐	☐
Ask and answer questions about changes in my life (Ex. 4)	☐	☐	☐
Describe personal goals (Ex. 5)	☐	☐	☐
Discuss and decide how to accomplish goals (Ex. 5)	☐	☐	☐

1 DISCUSSION The weekend

A GROUP WORK Find out what your classmates are doing this weekend.
Ask for details about each person's plans.

Name	Plans	Details

A: What are you going to do this weekend?
B: I'm watching a soccer game on Sunday.
C: Who's playing?

B GROUP WORK Whose weekend plans sound the best? Why?

2 ROLE PLAY Inviting a friend

Student A: Invite Student B to one of the events from Exercise 1. Say where and when it is.

Student B: Student A invites you out. Accept and ask for more information, or refuse and give an excuse.

Change roles and try the role play again.

3 LISTENING Matthew isn't here.

▶ Listen to the phone conversations. Write down the messages.

1

Message for: _____

Caller: _____

Message: _____

_____

_____

2

Message for: _____

Caller: _____

Message: _____

_____

_____

4 SURVEY Changes

A CLASS ACTIVITY Go around the class and find this information.
Write a classmate's name only once. Ask follow-up questions.

Find someone who . . .	Name
1. doesn't wear glasses anymore	
2. goes out more often these days	
3. got his or her hair cut last month	
4. got married last year	
5. has changed schools recently	
6. has gotten a part-time job recently	
7. has started a new hobby	
8. is happier these days	

B CLASS ACTIVITY Compare your information.
Who in the class has changed the most?

5 SPEAKING Setting goals

Check (✓) the goals you have and add two more. Then choose one goal.
Plan how to accomplish it with a partner.

☐ get into a good school   ☐ move to a new city   ☐ live a long time
☐ have more free time   ☐ own my own apartment ☐ _____
☐ have more friends   ☐ travel a lot more   ☐ _____

A: I'd like to have more free time.
B: How are you going to do that?

WHAT'S NEXT?

Look at your Self-assessment again. Do you need to review anything?

This page is intentionally left blank

Interchange activities

STUDENT A

A PAIR WORK How many differences can you find between your picture here and your partner's picture? Ask questions like these to find the differences.

How many people are standing / sitting / wearing . . . / holding a drink? Who?

What color is . . . 's T-shirt / sweater / hair?

Does . . . wear glasses / have a beard / have long hair?

What does . . . look like?

Picture 1

Leon

Elliott

Daniel

Joanna

Isla

Megan

B CLASS ACTIVITY How many differences are there in the pictures?
"In picture 1, Daniel's T-shirt is . . . In picture 2, it's . . ."

STUDENT B

A PAIR WORK How many differences can you find between your picture here and your partner's picture? Ask questions like these to find the differences.

How many people are standing / sitting / wearing . . . / holding a drink? Who?

What color is . . .'s T-shirt / sweater / hair?

Does . . . wear glasses / have a beard / have long hair?

What does . . . look like?

Picture 2

Leon

Elliott

Daniel

Joanna

Isla

Megan

B CLASS ACTIVITY How many differences are there in the pictures?
"In picture 1, Daniel's shirt is . . . In picture 2, it's . . ."

A PAIR WORK How much fun does your partner have? Interview him or her. Write the number of points using this scale.

never = 1 point
1–3 times = 2 points

4–7 times = 3 points
8 or more times = 4 points

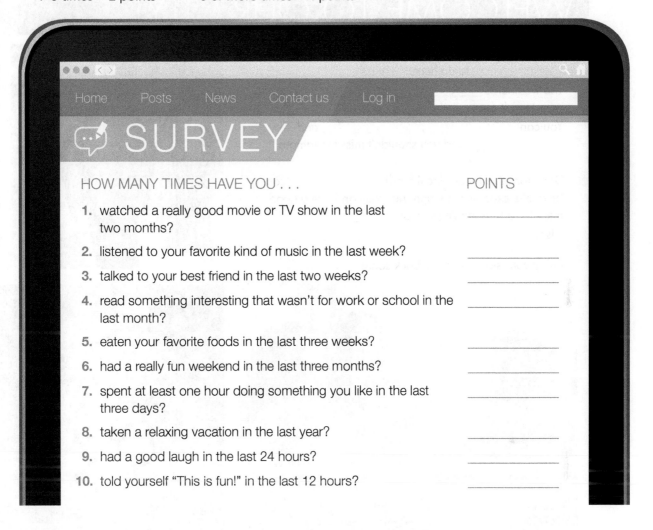

SURVEY

HOW MANY TIMES HAVE YOU . . .   **POINTS**

1. watched a really good movie or TV show in the last two months? _____
2. listened to your favorite kind of music in the last week? _____
3. talked to your best friend in the last two weeks? _____
4. read something interesting that wasn't for work or school in the last month? _____
5. eaten your favorite foods in the last three weeks? _____
6. had a really fun weekend in the last three months? _____
7. spent at least one hour doing something you like in the last three days? _____
8. taken a relaxing vacation in the last year? _____
9. had a good laugh in the last 24 hours? _____
10. told yourself "This is fun!" in the last 12 hours? _____

B GROUP WORK Add up your partner's points. Tell the group how much fun your partner has and why.

10–19 = You don't have enough fun. You should try to do things you enjoy more often! Stop and smell the roses!

20–29 = You have fun sometimes, but you need to do it more often. Continue to take time to do the things that you like.

30–40 = You know how to have fun! You know how to have a good time and enjoy life. Keep it up!

"Ellen has fun sometimes. She watches her favorite TV show once a week and takes a vacation twice a year. But she never reads anything she really likes – only the things she has to read for school."

C CLASS ACTIVITY Do you think your partner needs to have more fun? In what way?

"I think Ellen needs to have more fun in her life. She needs to spend more time doing things she likes. And she needs to eat her favorite foods more often. She also . . ."

A PAIR WORK You want to attract more visitors to your city or town. Complete the sentences below and add one more sentence to write a guide for tourists.

WELCOME TO OUR CITY!

LOGIN / REGISTER

It's a really _____ place and you will find _____ to do here.

The weather is _____ and the best times of the year to visit are _____ and _____.

You can _____, _____, and _____, and you shouldn't miss the famous _____!

Don't forget to try our local food! _____ can be a little expensive, though, but you can have a good meal for a reasonable price at _____.

Also, _____.

Enjoy your stay and come back soon!

B CLASS ACTIVITY Read your guide to the class. Ask follow-up questions to learn more.

What is the first place you should visit?

What is an exciting place to have fun on a Saturday night?

What is a relaxing place to visit on a Sunday morning?

What is a quiet place to study or do some work?

What is a really beautiful area that you shouldn't miss?

What is a dangerous area that you should avoid?

What places are usually too crowded?

Where can you exercise outdoors?

What fun things can you do for free?

Where's a popular place to meet?

C CLASS ACTIVITY Which are your two favorite guides? Which details did you find especially interesting about them?

A GROUP WORK Play the board game. Follow these instructions.

1. Write your initials on small pieces of paper. These are your game pieces.
2. Take turns by tossing a coin: If the coin lands face up, move two spaces. If the coin lands face down, move one space.
3. When you land on a space, ask two others in your group for advice.
4. The first person to cross the finish line is the winner.

A: I have the hiccups, Hiroto. What should I do?
B: Well, it's sometimes useful to hold your breath.
A: Thanks. What about you, Erica? What's your advice?
C: You should drink some water. That always works for me.

useful expressions

You should . . .
You could . . .
It's a good idea to . . .
It's important to . . .
I think it's useful to . . .

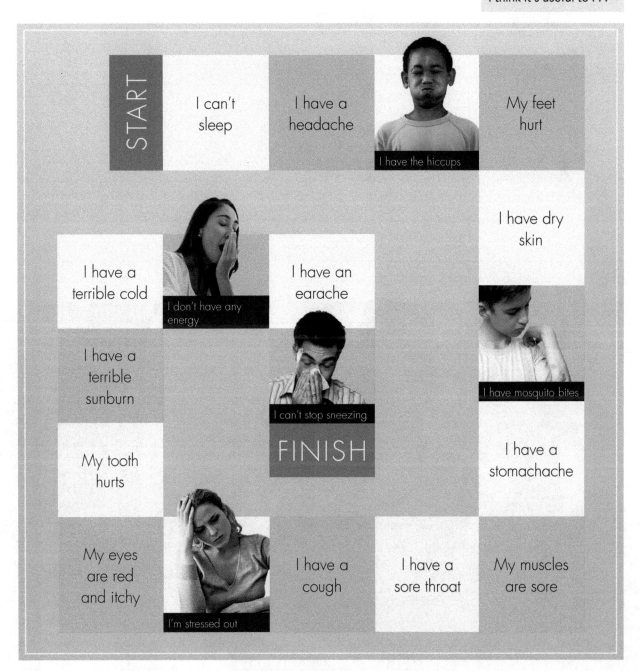

B CLASS ACTIVITY Who gave the best advice in your group? Tell the class.

A PAIR WORK Imagine your class is organizing a food festival with different food trucks. You and your classmate are responsible for one of the trucks. Choose a name for your truck. Write it at the top of the menu. Then, write the food and drinks you'd like to sell at your truck. Then write the prices.

B GROUP WORK Trade your menus with another pair. Order food and drinks from their menu, and then leave some suggestions about the menu on the message board.

_____
(write the name of your food truck here)

FOOD	PRICE

DRINKS	PRICE

CUSTOMERS' SUGGESTIONS

A PAIR WORK Take turns asking and answering these questions. Check (✓) the answer you think is correct for each question. Then write two more questions and answers.

World Knowledge Quiz

1. Which place is the wettest?	☐ Kaua'i, Hawai'i	☐ Manaus, Brazil	☐ Emei Shan, China
2. Which country is the hottest?	☐ Algeria	☐ Libya	☐ Somalia
3. Which country is closest to the equator?	☐ Colombia	☐ India	☐ Malaysia
4. Which animal is the biggest?	☐ a bison	☐ an elephant	☐ a blue whale
5. Which animal lives the longest?	☐ an elephant	☐ a tortoise	☐ a green iguana
6. Which mountain range is the longest?	☐ the Andes	☐ the Himalayas	☐ the Rockies
7. Which planet is the smallest?	☐ Earth	☐ Mercury	☐ Venus
8. Which planet is the largest?	☐ Jupiter	☐ Neptune	☐ Saturn
9. Which city is the oldest?	☐ Beijing, China	☐ Luxor, Egypt	☐ Rome, Italy
10. Which metal is the heaviest?	☐ aluminum	☐ gold	☐ silver

11. _____ _____ _____ _____
12. _____ _____ _____ _____

Manaus, Brazil

Emei Shan, China

Kaua'i, Hawai'i

1. Kaua'i, Hawai'i 6. the Andes
2. Lybia 7. Mercury
3. Colombia 8. Jupiter
4. a blue whale 9. Luxor, Egypt
5. a tortoise 10. gold

B PAIR WORK Check your answers. You and your partner get a point for every correct answer.

C CLASS ACTIVITY Ask your classmates your two questions. Get a point for every question nobody can answer correctly.

CLASS ACTIVITY What are your classmates' plans for the weekend?
Add two activities to the list. Then go around the class and find
people who are going to do these things. For each question,
ask for more information and take notes.

Find someone who's going to . . .	Name	Notes
go to a party		
go out of town		
go shopping		
see a live performance		
see/watch a movie		
see/watch a game		
meet friends		
visit relatives		
clean the house		
study for a test		

A: Samira, are you going to a party this weekend?
B: Yes, I am.
A: Where is the party going to be?
B: At my friend Lila's place. She's having a party to celebrate her birthday.

A **PAIR WORK** Talk with your partner and complete this chart with two ideas for each question – your idea and your partner's idea.

What is . . .	You	Your partner
something you plan to do next year?		
something you aren't going to do next year?		
something you hope to buy in the next year?		
something you would like to change about yourself?		
something you would like to learn?		
a place you would like to visit someday?		
a city you would like to live in someday?		
a job you would like to have?		
a goal you hope to achieve?		

A: What is something you plan to do next year?
B: Well, I'm going to travel to Morocco.
A: Oh, really? Where in Morocco?
B: I'm not sure yet! What about you?
What do you plan to do next year?

A: I'd like to get my own place.
B: Oh, really? Are you planning to rent an apartment?
A: No, actually I'm going to buy one.
B: Good for you!

B **GROUP ACTIVITY** Compare your information with another pair. Explain your goals and plans.

A: What are two things you plan to do next year?
B: Well, I'm going to visit Morocco, and Helena is going to get her own place.
C: That's right. I'm going to buy a small apartment. And you?
A: Well, I . . .

Grammar plus

1 Describing people page 59

> ■ Use *have* or *is* to describe eye and hair color: I **have** brown hair. = My hair **is** brown.
> He **has** blue eyes. = His eyes **are** blue.
>
> ■ Don't confuse *How* and *What* in questions: **How** tall are you? (NOT: ~~What tall are you?~~)
> **What** color is your hair? (NOT: ~~How color is your hair?~~)

Unscramble the questions. Then write answers using the phrases in the box.

| blond | brown eyes | contact lenses |
| ✓ tall and good-looking | 6 foot 2 | 26 – two years older than me |

A: brother   like   look   what   your   does
<u>What does your brother look like?</u>
B: <u>He's tall and good-looking.</u>
A: tall   is   how   he
_____
B: _____
A: he   does   glasses   wear
_____
B: _____
A: what   hair   color   his   is
_____
B: _____
A: he   does   blue   have   eyes
_____
B: _____
A: old   he   how   is
_____
B: _____

2 Modifiers with participles and prepositions page 62

> ■ Don't use a form of *be* in modifiers with participles: Sylvia is the woman **standing**
> near the window. (NOT: ~~Sylvia is the woman is standing near the window.~~)

Rewrite the conversations. Use the words in parentheses and *one* or *ones*.

1. **A:** Who's Carla?
   B: She's the woman in the red dress.

2. **A:** Who are your neighbors?
   B: They're the people with the baby.

3. **A:** Who's Jeff?
   B: He's the man wearing glasses.

A: <u>Which one is Carla?</u>_____ (which)
B: _____ (wearing)
A: _____ (which)
B: _____ (walking)
A: _____ (which)
B: _____ (with)

1 Present perfect; *already, yet* [page 65]

> ■ Use the present perfect for actions that happened some time in the past.
>
> ■ Use *yet* in questions and negative statements: Have you checked your email **yet**? No, I haven't turned on my computer **yet**. Use *already* in affirmative statements: I've **already** checked my email.

A Complete the conversations with the present perfect of the verbs in parentheses and short answers.

1. **A:** _____Has_____ Leslie _____called_____ (call) you lately?

   B: No, she _____ (not call) me, but I _____ (get) some emails from her.

2. **A:** _____ you and Jan _____ (have) lunch yet?

   B: No, we _____. We're thinking of going to Tony's. _____ you _____ (try) it yet? Come with us.

   A: Thanks. I _____ (not eat) there yet, but I _____ (hear) it's pretty good.

B Look at things Matt said. Put the adverb in the correct place in the second sentence.

1. I'm very hungry. I haven't eaten _∧ *yet* (yet)
2. I don't need any groceries. I've gone shopping. (already)
3. What have you done? Have you been to the zoo? (yet)
4. I called my parents before dinner. I've talked to them. (already)

2 Present perfect vs. simple past [page 66]

> ■ Don't mention a specific time with the present perfect: I**'ve been** to a jazz club. Use the simple past to say when a past action happened: I **went** to a jazz club **last night**.

Complete the conversation using the present perfect or the simple past of the verbs in parentheses and short answers.

1. **A:** _____Did_____ you _____see_____ (see) the game last night? I really _____ (enjoy) it.

   B: Yes, I _____. It _____ (be) an amazing game. _____ you ever _____ (go) to a game?

   A: No, I _____. I _____ never _____ (be) to the stadium. But I'd love to go!

   B: Maybe we can go to a game next year.

2. **A:** _____ you ever _____ (be) to Franco's Restaurant?

   B: Yes, I _____. My friend and I _____ (eat) there last weekend. How about you?

   A: No, I _____. But I _____ (hear) it's very good.

   B: Oh, yes – it's excellent!

3 *For* and *since* [page 67]

> ■ Use *for* + a period of time to describe how long a present condition has been true: We've been in New York **for two months**. (= We arrived two months ago.)
>
> ■ Use *since* + a point in time to describe when a present condition started: We've been here **since August**. (= We've been here from August to now.)

Choose the correct word.

1. I bought my car almost 10 years ago. I've had it **for / since** almost 10 years.
2. The Carters moved to Seattle six months ago. They've lived there **for / since** six months.
3. I've wanted to see that movie **for / since** a long time. It's been in theaters **for / since** March.

UNIT 11

1 Adverbs before adjectives page 73

> ■ Use *a/an* with (adverb) + adjective + singular noun: It's **a very modern city**. It's **an expensive city**. Don't use *a/an* with (adverb) + adjective: It's **really interesting**. (NOT: ~~It's a really interesting.~~)

Read the sentences. Add *a* or *an* where it's necessary to complete the sentences.

1. Brasília is ∧ extremely modern city.
   an

2. Seoul is very interesting place.

3. Santiago is pretty exciting city to visit.

4. Montreal is beautiful city, and it's fairly old.

5. London has really busy airport.

2 Conjunctions page 73

> ■ Use *and* for additional information: The food is delicious, **and** it's not expensive.
> ■ Use *but, though,* and *however* for contrasting information: The food is delicious, **but** it's very expensive./The food is delicious. It's expensive, **though/however**.

Choose the correct word.

1. Spring in my city is pretty nice, **and / but** it gets extremely hot in summer.
2. There are some great museums. They're always crowded, **and / however**.
3. There are a lot of interesting stores, **and / but** many of them aren't expensive.
4. There are many amazing restaurants, **and / but** some are closed in August.
5. My city is a great place to visit. Don't come in summer, **but / though**!

3 Modal verbs *can* and *should* page 75

> ■ Use *can* to talk about things that are possible: Where **can** I get some nice souvenirs? Use *should* to suggest things that are good to do: You **should** try the local restaurants.
> ■ Use the base form with *can* and *should* – not the infinitive: Where **can I get** some nice souvenirs? (NOT: ~~Where can I to get . . .?~~) You **should try** the local restaurants. (NOT: ~~You should to try . . .~~)

Complete the conversation with *can, can't, should,* or *shouldn't*.

A: I ____can't____ decide where to go on vacation. _____ I go to Costa Rica or Hawaii?

B: You _____ definitely visit Costa Rica.

A: Really? What can I see there?

B: Well, San Jose is an exciting city. You _____ miss the Museo del Oro. That's the gold museum, and you _____ see beautiful animals made of gold.

A: OK. What else _____ I do there?

B: Well, you _____ visit the museum on Mondays. It's closed then. But you _____ definitely visit the rain forest. It's amazing!

1 Adjective + infinitive; noun + infinitive page 79

> ■ In negative statements, *not* comes before the infinitive: With a cold, it's important **not to exercise** too hard. (NOT: ~~With a cold, it's important to don't exercise too hard.~~)

Rewrite the sentences using the words in parentheses. Add *not* when necessary.

1. For a bad headache, you should relax and close your eyes. (a good idea)
   <u>It's a good idea to relax and close your eyes when you have a headache.</u>

2. You should put some cold tea on that sunburn. (sometimes helpful)
   _____

3. For a backache, you should take some pain medicine. (important)
   _____

4. For a cough, you shouldn't drink milk. (important)
   _____

5. For a cold, you should take a hot bath. (sometimes helpful)
   _____

6. When you feel stressed, you shouldn't drink a lot of coffee. (a good idea)
   _____

2 Modal verbs *can*, *could*, and *may* for requests; suggestions page 81

> ■ In requests, *can*, *could*, and *may* have the same meaning. *May* is a little more formal than *can* and *could*.

Number the lines of the conversation. Then write the conversation below.

_____ Hi. Yes, please. What do you suggest for itchy skin?

_____ Here you are. Can I help you with anything else?

_____ Sure I can. You should see a dentist!

___1___ Hello. May I help you?

_____ You should try this lotion.

_____ Yes. Can you suggest something for a toothache?

_____ OK. And could I have a bottle of pain medicine?

A: <u>Hello. May I help you?</u>
B: _____
A: _____
B: _____
A: _____
B: _____
A: _____

1 *So, too, neither, either* page 87

> ■ Use *so* or *too* after an affirmative statement: I'm crazy about sushi. **So am I./I am, too.**
>
> ■ Use *neither* or *not either* after a negative statement: I don't like fast food. **Neither do I./I don't either.**
>
> ■ With *so* and *neither*, the verb comes before the subject: **So am I.** (NOT: So I am.) **Neither do I.** (NOT: Neither I do.)

A Choose the correct response to show that B agrees with A.

1. **A:** I'm in the mood for something salty.
   B: (I am, too.) / I do, too.
2. **A:** I can't stand fast food.
   B: Neither do I. / I can't either.
3. **A:** I really like Korean food.
   B: So do I. / I am, too.
4. **A:** I don't eat French food very often.
   B: I do, too. / I don't either.
5. **A:** I'm not crazy about chocolate.
   B: I am, too. / Neither am I.

B Write responses to show agreement with these statements.

1. **A:** I'm not a very good cook.
   B: _____
2. **A:** I love french fries.
   B: _____
3. **A:** I can't eat very spicy food.
   B: _____
4. **A:** I never eat bland food.
   B: _____
5. **A:** I can make delicious desserts.
   B: _____

2 Modal verbs *would* and *will* for requests page 89

> ■ Don't confuse *like* and *would like. Would like* means "want."
>
> ■ You can also use *I'll have . . .* when ordering in a restaurant to mean *I will have . . .*

Complete the conversation with *would, I'd,* or *I'll.*

A: ____Would____ you like to order now?

B: Yes, please. _____ have the shrimp curry.

A: _____ you like noodles or rice with that?

B: Hmm, _____ have rice.

A: And _____ you like a salad, too?

B: No, thanks.

A: _____ you like anything else?

B: Yes, _____ like a cup of green tea.

1 Comparisons with adjectives page 93

> ■ Use the comparative form (adjective + *-er* or *more* + adjective) to compare two people, places, or things: Which river is **longer**, the Nile or the Amazon? The Nile is **longer than** the Amazon. Use the superlative form (*the* + adjective + *-est* or *the most* + adjective) to compare three or more people, places, or things: Which river is **the longest**: the Nile, the Amazon, or the Mississippi? The Nile is **the longest** river in the world.
>
> ■ You can use a comparative or superlative without repeating the noun: Which country is **larger**, Canada or China? Canada is **larger**. What's the highest waterfall in the world? Angel Falls is **the highest**.

Write questions with the words. Then look at the underlined words, and write the answers.

1. Which desert / dry / the Sahara or <u>the Atacama</u>?
   Q: <u>Which desert is drier, the Sahara or the Atacama?</u>
   A: <u>The Atacama is drier than the Sahara.</u>

2. Which island / large / <u>Greenland</u>, New Guinea, or Honshu?
   Q: _____
   A: _____

3. Which island / small / New Guinea or <u>Honshu</u>?
   Q: _____
   A: _____

4. Which U.S. city / large / Los Angeles, Chicago, or <u>New York</u>?
   Q: _____
   A: _____

5. Which ocean / deep / the Atlantic or <u>the Pacific</u>?
   Q: _____
   A: _____

2 Questions with *how* page 96

> ■ Use *high* to describe mountains and waterfalls: How **high** is Mount Fuji? Angel Falls is 979 meters **high**. Use *tall* to describe buildings: How **tall** is the Empire State Building? (NOT: ~~How high is the Empire State Building?~~)

Complete the questions with the phrases in the box. There is one extra phrase.

How big	How cold	✓ How deep	How high	How tall

1. **Q:** <u>How deep</u> is Lake Baikal? **A:** It's 1,642 meters (5,387 feet) at its deepest point.
2. **Q:** _____ is Alaska? **A:** It's 1,717,900 square kilometers (663,300 square miles).
3. **Q:** _____ is Denali? **A:** It's 6,190 meters (20,310 feet) high.
4. **Q:** _____ is the Tokyo Skytree? **A:** It is 634 meters (2,080 feet) tall.

UNIT 15

1 Future with present continuous and *be going to* `page 101`

> - Use the present continuous to talk about something that is happening now: What **are** you **doing**? I'**m studying**. You can also use the present continuous with time expressions to talk about the future: What **are** you **doing tomorrow**? I'**m working.**
> - Use *be going to* to talk about the future: I'**m going to** see an old school friend tomorrow.

A Read the sentences. Are they present or future? Write **P** or **F**.

1. Why are you wearing shorts? It's cold. ___P___
2. What are you wearing to the party on Friday? _____
3. What are you doing this weekend? _____
4. What are you doing? Can you please see who's at the door? _____
5. Are you going to see a movie tonight? _____

B Complete the conversations. Use *be going to*.

1. **A:** What _____are_____ you and Tony going to _____do_____ (do) tonight?
   B: We _____ (try) the new Chinese restaurant. Do you want to come?
   A: I'd love to. What time _____ you _____ (go)?
   B: We _____ (meet) at Tony's house at 7:00. And don't forget an umbrella. The weather forecast says it _____ (rain) tonight.
2. **A:** Where _____ you _____ (go) on vacation this year?
   B: I _____ (visit) my cousins in Paris. It _____ (be) great!
   A: Well, I _____ (not go) anywhere this year. I _____ (stay) home.
   B: That's not so bad. Just think about all the money you _____ (save)!

2 Messages with *tell* and *ask* `page 103`

> - In messages with a request, use the infinitive of the verb: Please ask her **to meet** me at noon. (NOT: ~~Please ask her meet me at noon.~~)
> - In messages with negative infinitives, *not* goes before *to* in the infinitive: Could you ask him **not to be** late? (NOT: ~~Could you ask him to don't be late?~~)

Read the messages. Ask someone to pass them on. Use the words in parentheses.

1. Message: Patrick – We don't have class tomorrow. (please)
   <u>Please tell Patrick that we don't have class tomorrow.</u>
2. Message: Ana – Wait for me after class. (would)
   _____
3. Message: Alex – The concert on Saturday has been canceled. (would)
   _____
4. Message: Sarah – Don't forget to return the book to the library. (could)
   _____

UNIT 16

1 Describing changes page 107

> ■ You can use several tenses to describe change – present tense, past tense, and present perfect.

A Complete the sentences with the information in the box. Use the present perfect of the verbs given.

buy a house   change her hairstyle   join a gym   start looking for a new job

1. Chris and Brittany _____. Their apartment was too small.
2. Josh _____. The one he has now is too stressful.
3. Shawna _____. Everyone says it's more stylish.
4. Max _____. He feels healthier now.

B Rewrite the sentences using the present tense and the words in parentheses.

1. Holly doesn't wear jeans anymore. _She wears dresses._____ (dresses)
2. They don't live in the city anymore. _____ (in the suburbs)
3. Jackie isn't so shy anymore. _____ (more outgoing)
4. I don't eat greasy food anymore. _____ (healthier food)

2 Verb + infinitive page 109

> ■ Use the infinitive after a verb to describe future plans or things you want to happen:
> I **want to learn** Spanish.

Complete the conversation with the verbs in parentheses in the correct form.

A: Hey, Zach. What _are you going to do_____ (go / do) after graduation?
B: Well, I _____ (plan / stay) here in the city for a few months.
A: Really? I _____ (want / go) home. I'm ready for my mom's cooking.
B: I understand that, but my boss says I can keep my job for the summer. So
     I _____ (want / work) a lot of hours because I
     _____ (hope / make) enough money for a new car.
A: But you don't need a car in the city.
B: I _____ (not plan / be) here for very long. In the
     fall, I _____ (go / drive) across the country. I really
     _____ (want / live) in California.
A: California? Where in California _____ (like / live)?
B: In Hollywood, of course. I _____ (go / be) a movie star!

Grammar plus answer key

Unit 9

1 Describing people
A: How tall is he?
B: He's 6 foot 2.
A: Does he wear glasses?
B: No, he doesn't. He wears contact lenses.
A: What color is his hair?
B: He has blond hair.
A: Does he have blue eyes?
B: No, he has brown eyes.
A: How old is he?
B: He's 26 – two years older than me.

2 Modifiers with participles and prepositions
1. B: She's the one wearing a red dress.
2. A: Which ones are your neighbors?
   B: They're the ones walking with the baby.
3. A: Which one is Jeff?
   B: He's the one with glasses.

Unit 10

1 Present perfect; *already, yet*
A
1. B: No, she **hasn't called** me, but I**'ve gotten** some emails from her.
2. A: **Have** you and Jan **had** lunch yet?
   B: No, we **haven't**. We're thinking of going to Tony's. **Have** you **tried** it yet? Come with us.
   A: Thanks. I **haven't eaten** there yet, but I**'ve heard** it's pretty good.

B
2. I've **already** gone shopping.
3. Have you been to the zoo **yet**?
4. I've **already** talked to them./I've talked to them **already**.

2 Present perfect vs. simple past
1. A: Did you see the game last night? I really **enjoyed** it.
   B: Yes, I **did**. It **was** an amazing game. **Have** you ever **gone** to a game?
   A: No, I **haven't**. I**'ve** never **been** to the stadium. But I'd love to go!
   B: Maybe we can go to a game next year.
2. A: **Have** you ever **been** to Franco's Restaurant?
   B: Yes, I **have**. My friend and I **ate** there last weekend. How about you?
   A: No, I **haven't**. But I**'ve heard** it's very good.
   B: Oh, yes – it's excellent!

3 *For* and *since*
1. I've had it **for** almost 10 years.
2. They've lived there **for** six months.
3. I've wanted to see that movie **for** a long time. It's been in theaters **since** March.

Unit 11

1 Adverbs before adjectives
2. Seoul is **a** very interesting place.
3. Santiago is **a** pretty exciting city to visit.
4. Montreal is **a** beautiful city, and it's fairly old.
5. London has **a** really busy airport.

2 Conjunctions
1. Spring in my city is pretty nice, **but** it gets extremely hot in summer.
2. There are some great museums. They're always crowded, **however**.
3. There are a lot of interesting stores, **and** many of them aren't expensive.
4. There are many amazing restaurants, **but** some are closed in August.
5. My city is a great place to visit. Don't come in summer, **though**!

3 Modal verbs *can* and *should*
A: I **can't** decide where to go on vacation. **Should** I go to Costa Rica or Hawaii?
B: You **should** definitely visit Costa Rica.
A: Really? What can I see there?
B: Well, San Jose is an exciting city. You **shouldn't** miss the Museo del Oro. That's the gold museum, and you **can** see beautiful animals made of gold.
A: OK. What else **can / should** I do there?
B: Well, you **can't** visit the museum on Mondays. It's closed then. But you **should** definitely visit the rain forest. It's amazing!

Unit 12

1 Adjective + infinitive; noun + infinitive
Possible answers:
2. For a sunburn, **it's sometimes helpful to put** some cold tea on it.
3. For a backache, **it's important to take** some pain medicine.
4. For a cough, **it's important not to drink** milk.
5. For a cold, **it's sometimes helpful to take** a hot bath.
6. When you feel stressed, **it's a good idea not to drink** a lot of coffee.

2 Modal verbs *can, could,* and *may* for requests; suggestions
2. Yes, please. What do you suggest for itchy skin?
3. You should try this lotion.
4. OK. And could I have a bottle of pain medicine?
5. Here you are. Can I help you with anything else?
6. Yes. Can you suggest something for a toothache?
7. Sure I can. You should see a dentist!

Unit 13

1 *So, too, neither, either*

A
2. B: I can't either.
3. B: So do I.
4. B: I don't either.
5. B: Neither am I.

B
1. B: I'm not either./Neither am I.
2. B: I do, too./So do I.
3. B: I can't either./Neither can I.
4. B: I don't either./Neither do I.
5. B: I can, too./So can I.

2 Modal verbs *would* and *will* for requests

B: I'll
A: Would
B: I'll
A: would
A: Would
B: I'd

Unit 14

1 **Comparisons with adjectives**
2. Q: Which island is the largest: Greenland, New Guinea, or Honshu?
   A: Greenland is the largest.
3. Q: Which island is smaller, New Guinea or Honshu?
   A: Honshu is smaller than New Guinea.
4. Q: Which U.S. city is the largest: Los Angeles, Chicago, or New York?
   A: New York is the largest.
5. Q: Which ocean is deeper, the Atlantic or the Pacific?
   A: The Pacific is deeper than the Atlantic.

2 **Questions with *how***
2. How big
3. How high
4. How tall

Unit 15

1 **Future with present continuous and *be going to***

A
2. F
3. F
4. P
5. F

B
1. B: We**'re going to try** the new Chinese restaurant. Do you want to come?
   A: I'd love to. What time **are** you **going to go**?
   B: We**'re going to meet** at Tony's house at 7:00. And don't forget an umbrella. The weather forecast says it**'s going to rain** tonight.
2. A: Where **are you going to go** on vacation this year?
   B: I**'m going to visit** my cousins in Paris. It**'s going to be** great!
   A: Well, I**'m not going to go** anywhere this year. I**'m going to stay** home.
   B: That's not so bad. Just think about all the money you**'re going to save**!

2 **Messages with *tell* and *ask***
2. Would you ask Ana to wait for me after class?
3. Would you tell Alex (that) the concert on Saturday has been canceled?
4. Could you tell Sarah not to forget to return the book to the library?

Unit 16

1 **Describing changes**

A
1. Chris and Brittany **have bought a house**.
2. Josh **has started looking for a new job**.
3. Shawn **has changed her hairstyle**.
4. Max **has joined a gym**.

B
2. They live in the suburbs.
3. Jackie/She is more outgoing.
4. I eat healthier food now.

2 **Verb + infinitive**
B: Well, I **plan to stay** here in the city for a few months.
A: Really? I **want to go** home. I'm ready for my mom's cooking.
B: I understand that, but my boss says I can keep my job for the summer. So I **want to work** a lot of hours because I **hope to make** enough money for a new car.
A: But you don't need a car in the city.
B: I **don't plan to be** here for very long. In the fall, I**'m going to drive** across the country. I really **want to live** in California.
A: California? Where in California **would you like to live**?
B: In Hollywood, of course. I**'m going to be** a movie star!

Credits

The authors and publishers acknowledge the following sources of copyright material and are grateful for the permissions granted. While every effort has been made, it has not always been possible to identify the sources of all the material used, or to trace all copyright holders. If any omissions are brought to our notice, we will be happy to include the appropriate acknowledgements on reprinting and in the next update to the digital edition, as applicable.

Keys: E = Exercise; T = Top, B = Below, TR = Top Right, TL = Top Left, BR = Below Right, BL = Below Left, C = Centre, CR = Centre Right, CL = Centre Left, L = Left, R = Right, BC = Below Centre, B/G = Background.

Illustrations

337 Jon (KJA Artists): 17(T); **Mark Duffin**: 17(B), 80; **Thomas Girard** (Good Illustration): 50, 64, 66, 78(B), 108, 116–117; **Daniel Gray-Barnett**: 51, 57, 92; **Quino Marin** (The Organisation): 17(C), 18, 56, 70, 120; **Gavin Reece** (New Division): 2, 3, 5, 61, 123, 124; **Paul Williams** (Sylvie Poggio Artists): 60, 78(T).

Photos

Back cover (woman with whiteboard): Jenny Acheson/Stockbyte/GettyImages; Back cover (whiteboard): Nemida/GettyImages; Back cover (man using phone): Betsie Van Der Meer/Taxi/GettyImages; Back cover (woman smiling): PeopleImages.com/DigitalVision/GettyImages; Back cover (name tag): Tetra Images/GettyImages; Back cover (handshake): David Lees/Taxi/GettyImages; p. v: Caiaimage/Chris Ryan/GettyImages; p. 58 (header), p. viii (Unit 9): Tom Merton/Caiaimage/GettyImages; p. 58 (long hair): Portra Images/DigitalVision/GettyImages; p. 58 (short hair): KidStock/Blend Images/GettyImages; p. 58 (straight hair): Rick Gomez/Blend Images/GettyImages; p. 58 (curly hair): Rainer Holz/Westend61/GettyImages; p. 58 (bald): wickedpix/iStock/Getty Images Plus/GettyImages; p. 58 (mustache and beard): shapecharge/E+/GettyImages; p. 58 (young): RedChopsticks/GettyImages; p. 58 (middle aged): Caiaimage/Chris Ryan/OJO+/GettyImages; p. 58 (elderly): David Sucsy/E+/GettyImages; p. 58 (handsome): Yuri_Arcurs/iStock/Getty Images Plus/GettyImages; p. 58 (good looking): Wavebreakmedia Ltd/Getty Images Plus/GettyImages; p. 58 (pretty): AntonioGuillem/iStock/Getty Images Plus/GettyImages; p. 58 (short): Ana Abejon/E+/GettyImages; p. 58 (fairly short): DRB Images, LLC/E+/GettyImages; p. 58 (medium height): 4x6/E+/GettyImages; p. 58 (pretty tall): momentimages/GettyImages; p. 58 (very tall): Photodisc/Stockbyte/GettyImages; p. 59: Tim Robberts/Taxi/GettyImages; p. 61 (Boho): Christian Vierig/WireImage/GettyImages; p. 61 (Classic): aleksle/E+/GettyImages; p. 61 (Hipster): SeanShot/E+/GettyImages; p. 61 (Streetwear): Peter Muller/Cultura/GettyImages; p. 63 (TL): Robert Cornelius/Hulton Archive/GettyImages; p. 63 (BL): Dougal Waters/DigitalVision/GettyImages; p. 63 (TR): NASA/Getty Images North America/GettyImages; p. 63 (BR): Tim Stewart News/REX/Shutterstock; p. 64 (header), p. viii (Unit 10): Paul Andrew Lawrence/Visuals Unlimited, Inc./GettyImages; p. 64 (theme park): Danielle Gali/AWL Images/GettyImages; p. 64 (go dancing): Diverse Images/UIG/GettyImages; p. 64 (space centre): Hiroyuki Matsumoto/Photographer's Choice/GettyImages; p. 64 (Cuban food): 424846/Hemera/Getty Images Plus/GettyImages; p. 64 (alligator): LaDora Sims/Moment/GettyImages; p. 67: Masaaki Toyoura/The Image Bank/GettyImages; p. 68: Dan Dalton/Caiaimage/GettyImages; p. 69 (TR): Anna_Shepulova/iStock/Getty Images Plus/GettyImages; p. 69 (CL): James Devaney/WireImage/GettyImages; p. 69 (CR): Simon Brown NI/Photolibrary/GettyImages; p. 69 (BL): Romilly Lockyer/Photographer's Choice/GettyImages; p. 71: CoCam/iStock/Getty Images Plus/GettyImages; p. 72 (header), p. viii (Unit 11): Tetra Images/GettyImages; p. 72 (beautiful): Sylvain Sonnet/GettyImages; p. 72 (ugly): donvictorio/iStock/Getty Images Plus/GettyImages; p. 72 (BR): Jane Sweeney/AWL Images/GettyImages; p. 73: 2630ben/iStock/Getty Images Plus/GettyImages; p. 74 (CR): Andrew Bain/Lonely Planet Images/GettyImages; p. 74 (photo 1): Michele Falzone/The Image Bank/GettyImages; p. 74 (photo 2): seng chye teo/Moment/GettyImages; p. 74 (photo 3): WitR/iStock/Getty Images Plus/GettyImages; p. 74 (photo 4): Photo by Hanneke Luijting/Moment/GettyImages; p. 74 (photo 5): f11photo/iStock/Getty Images Plus/GettyImages; p. 74 (photo 6): Panoramic Images/Panoramic Images/GettyImages; p. 75 (TR): Julius Reque/Moment Mobile/GettyImages; p. 75 (CR): Christian Kober/robertharding/GettyImages; p. 75 (Jason): svetikd/E+/GettyImages; p. 75 (Claudia): Hill Street Studios/Blend Images/GettyImages; p. 76 (TR): Eric Lo/Moment/GettyImages; p. 76 (BR): 153photostudio/iStock/Getty Images Plus/GettyImages; p. 77 (TR): Manfred Gottschalk/Lonely Planet Images/GettyImages; p. 77 (CL): Jeremy Woodhouse/Photographer's Choice RF/GettyImages; p. 77 (CR): Kimberley Coole/Lonely Planet Images/GettyImages; p. 78 (header), p. viii (Unit 12): Paul Bradbury/Caiaimage/GettyImages; p. 79 (sore throat): BSIP/UIG/Universal Images Group/GettyImages; p. 79 (fever): Tom Le Goff/DigitalVision/GettyImages; p. 79 (toothache): Eric Audras/ONOKY/GettyImages; p. 79 (burn): Jurgute/iStock/Getty Images Plus/GettyImages; p. 80: annebaek/E+/GettyImages; p. 81 (TR): Yuri_Arcurs/E+/GettyImages; p. 81 (BR): simarik/E+/GettyImages; p. 82: PeopleImages.com/DigitalVision/GettyImages; p. 83: rbiedermann/iStock/Getty Images Plus/GettyImages; p. 83 (B/G): Johnny Lye/iStock/Getty Images Plus/GettyImages; p. 85 (stomachache): IAN HOOTON/Science Photo Library/GettyImages; p. 85 (insect bite): BURGER/PHANIE/Canopy/GettyImages; p. 85 (nosebleed): LEA PATERSON/SCIENCE PHOTO LIBRARY/Science Photo Library/GettyImages; p. 85 (hiccups): Peopleimages/iStock/Getty Images Plus/GettyImages; p. 85 (CL): Image Source/Photodisc/GettyImages; p. 85 (C): Pascal Broze/ONOKY/GettyImages; p. 85 (CR): kali9/E+/GettyImages; p. 86 (header), p. viii (Unit 13): Hero Images/Hero Images/GettyImages; p. 86 (apple pie): John Montana/StockFood Creative/GettyImages; p. 86 (chocolate): Thomas Francois/iStock/Getty Images Plus; p. 86 (french fries): Rachel Weill/UpperCut Images/GettyImages; p. 86 (hamburger): Westend61/GettyImages; p. 86 (icecream cone): Oksana Dzhaketi/EyeEm/EyeEm/GettyImages; p. 86 (pasta): jon whitaker/Dorling Kindersley/GettyImages; p. 86 (sandwich): julie clancy/Moment/GettyImages; p. 86 (sushi): Foodcollection/GettyImages; p. 86 (BR): Cultura RM Exclusive/Matelly/Cultura Exclusive; p. 87 (bland): powerbeephoto/iStock/Getty Images Plus/GettyImages; p. 87 (delicious): Agnieszka Kirinicjanow/E+/GettyImages; p. 87 (greasy): Foodcollection/GettyImages; p. 87 (healthy): matka_Wariatka/iStock/Getty Images Plus/GettyImages; p. 87 (rich): Luzia Ellert/StockFood Creative/GettyImages; p. 87 (salty): magnetcreative/iStock/Getty Images Plus/GettyImages; p. 87 (spicy): Floortje/E+/GettyImages; p. 88 (board): Jon Schulte/E+/GettyImages;

p. 88 (B/G): Sonya_illustration/iStock/Getty Images Plus; p. 88 (BR): andresr/E+/Gettyimages; p. 89: NicoleArnoldPhotography/GettyImages; p. 90 (TR): Justin Geoffrey/Iconica/GettyImages; p. 90 (girl): Peopleimages/E+/GettyImages; p. 90 (burger): Yurika Yamada/EyeEm/EyeEm/GettyImages; p. 91: JGI/Jamie Grill/Blend Images/GettyImages; p. 92 (header), p. viii (Unit 14): Bjarki Reyr/Stone/GettyImages; p. 93: andresr/E+/GettyImages; p. 94 (L): Mint Images - Liesel Bockl/Mint Images RF/GettyImages; p. 94 (C): Celia Peterson/arabianEye/GettyImages; p. 94 (R): Dave and Les Jacobs/Kolostock/Blend Images/GettyImages; p. 95 (T): Witold Skrypczak/Lonely Planet Images/GettyImages; p. 95 (B): Stuart Westmorland/Photographer's Choice/GettyImages; p. 96: Al Rod/Stockbyte/GettyImages; p. 97 (TR): Canadian Space Agency/RADARSAT/NASA/Science Photo Library; p. 97 (CL): Australian Scenics/Photolibrary/GettyImages; p. 97 (BR): TERADAT SANTIVIVUT/E+/GettyImages; p. 99: itkin_photo/iStock/Getty Images Plus/GettyImages; p. 100 (header), p. viii (Unit 15): Diverse Images/UIG/Universal Images Group/GettyImages; p. 100 (CR): Westend61/GettyImages; p. 100 (BR): Hero Images/Hero Images/GettyImages; p. 102 (TR): Miroslav Georgijevic/Vetta/GettyImages; p. 102 (R): Ariel Skelley/Blend Images/GettyImages; p. 102 (Jake): Ariel Skelley/Blend Images/GettyImages; p. 102 (Caitlin): Joan Vicent Canto Roig/E+/GettyImages; p. 103: Robert Daly/Caiaimage/GettyImages; p. 105 (TR): Todor Tsvetkov/E+/GettyImages; p. 105 (CL): Tony Garcia/Image Source/GettyImages; p. 105 (CR): Getty Images/Staff/Getty Images News/GettyImages; p. 105 (BL): Cultura Exclusive/We Boldly Went/Cultura Exclusive/GettyImages; p. 106 (header), p. viii (Unit 16): AndreyPopov/iStock/Getty Images Plus/GettyImages; p. 106 (BR): Westend61/GettyImages; p. 107 (TR): franckreporter/E+/GettyImages; p. 107 (CR): Yagi Studio/DigitalVision/GettyImages; p. 107 (BR): Catherine Delahaye/Taxi/GettyImages; p. 109 (CR): Peopleimages/E+/GettyImages; p. 109 (BR): Caiaimage/Tom Merton/OJO+/GettyImages; p. 110 (TR): andresr/E+/GettyImages; p. 110 (CR): andresr/E+/GettyImages; p. 111 (TR): Michel Porro/Getty Images News/GettyImages; p. 111 (B): REMKO DE WAAL/Stringer/AFP/GettyImages; p. 112: Aksonov/Vetta/GettyImages; p. 113: Wavebreakmedia Ltd/Wavebreak Media/Getty Images Plus/GettyImages; p. 126 (TR): Erik Von Weber/Taxi/GettyImages; p. 126 (CR): Christian Kober/Photographer's Choice/GettyImages; p. 126 (CL): Inti St Clair/Blend Images/GettyImages; p. 127 (hiccups): Jupiterimages/Photolibrary/GettyImages; p. 127 (yawning): JGI/Jamie Grill/Blend Images/GettyImages; p. 127 (stressed): BSIP/UIG/Universal Images Group/GettyImages; p. 127 (mosquito bite): art-4-art/E+/GettyImages; p. 127 (sneezing): Compassionate Eye Foundation/David Oxberry/OJO Images Ltd/DigitalVision/GettyImages; p. 128: Hero Images/Hero Images/GettyImages; p. 129 (Kaua'i): M Swiet Productions/Moment/GettyImages; p. 129 (Manaus): Marcelo Andre/Photolibrary/GettyImages; p. 129 (B/G): © HO Soo Khim/Moment/GettyImages; p. 130 (L): JGI/Jamie Grill/Blend Images/GettyImages; p. 130 (CR): Hero Images/Hero Images/GettyImages; p. 130 (BR): Garry Wade/Taxi/GettyImages; p. 131 (CR): Jessica Peterson/GettyImages; p. 131 (TR): Nasser Mar/EyeEm/GettyImages.